FEMINIST LITERARY CRITICISM

Feminist Literary Criticism
Explorations in Theory

Josephine Donovan, *editor*

THE UNIVERSITY PRESS OF KENTUCKY

ISBN: 0-8131-1334-2

Library of Congress Catalog Card Number: 75-12081

Editorial and Sales Offices: Lexington, Kentucky 40506

if I'm lonely
it must be the loneliness
of waking first, of breathing
dawn's first cold breath on the city
of being the one awake
in a house wrapped in sleep

—Adrienne Rich

if they ask me my identity
what can I say but
I am the androgyne
I am the living mind you fail to describe
in your dead language
the lost noun, the verb surviving
only in the infinitive
the letters of my name are written under the lids
of the newborn child

—Adrienne Rich

CONTENTS

EDITOR'S PREFACE

This collection of essays on feminist literary criticism grew out of a symposium on feminism and literature that was held on the University of Kentucky campus, April 27-28, 1973, as part of the 1973 Kentucky Foreign Language Conference. Two of the essays included here were originally given as papers at that symposium, but have been modified for this collection. These are the dialogue by Carolyn Heilbrun and Catharine Stimpson, and the preface to Virginia Woolf's criticism by Barbara Currier Bell and Carol Ohmann. The essay by Dorin Schumacher was written after she participated in the symposium, and the two remaining pieces, the essay by Marcia Holly and Cheri Register's bibliographical survey, were done independently.

I have gathered these essays together to present an interpretation, and in some sense a defense, of feminist literary criticism, which, like its mother movement, is already much misunderstood and maligned. The essays are ordered for the reader who knows little about feminist criticism. Register's bibliographical essay provides an excellent interpretive introduction to the body of existing feminist criticism. Following are Schumacher's and Holly's theoretical discussions about assumptions behind traditional literary criticism that are being challenged by the new feminist critics. The Bell-Ohmann preface introduces Virginia Woolf's critical practice, which is both a neglected aspect of her work and an important antecedent to the current critical movement.

I have chosen to conclude the collection with a dialogue on feminist criticism by two distinguished feminist scholars, Professors Heilbrun and Stimpson. I think it appropriate to end, as it were, in the midst of discussion. For it seems that, like Gertrude Stein, feminist critics are not so much concerned with proposing answers as with wondering about the question itself. In this vein I have postscripted my own speculations about feminist criticism and its future.

AMERICAN FEMINIST LITERARY CRITICISM:
A BIBLIOGRAPHICAL INTRODUCTION

Cheri Register

A young woman is sitting on the bus reading Doris Lessing's *The Golden Notebook*. Her young male seat companion comments, "You must be into women's lib." At a workshop on sexism in education, an English teacher asks what she can give her seventh graders—in addition to *Little Women*—to counter the influence of *Double Date* and *Double Feature*. The members of a feminist collective circulate among themselves a well-worn volume of Sylvia Plath's poetry. The women's magazine *Redbook* prints an excerpt from Kate Chopin's *The Awakening*, which has been ignored since the controversy following its publication in 1899.[1]

Such incidents signal the emergence of *feminist criticism*, a new literary analysis based on the tenets of the American women's movement. This essay will define feminist criticism, explain how it operates, and show what political functions it performs.

The emergence of feminist criticism, like the mushrooming of its parent political movement, owes as much to spontaneous generation as to nationwide organization. Although the impetus to read Doris Lessing comes via the informal feminist grapevine, the reader must depend on her personal response to the book and evaluate it in terms of her own tastes and priorities. There has been no predetermined and generally accepted analytical method to apply to it. However, instructors of female studies have exchanged suggestions about book selection, and they have now begun to share ideas about critical approaches for classroom discussion, both in publications and at conferences.

Formulation of the feminist criticism already operant has been undertaken mainly by junior faculty women and graduate students in college and university English departments, which should come as no surprise. The greatest proportion of women in English departments is clustered at the "junior" level.[2] In fact, appeals for a new feminist criticism are often coupled with agitation against discriminatory hiring and admissions policies. Feminists believe that the predominance of men in academic positions has given rise to a sex-biased literary standard.

The formation of the Modern Language Association's Commission on the Status of Women in 1970 marks the beginning of an organized critical effort. It has put academic feminists in contact with one another and resulted in the publication of the *Female Studies* series, seven volumes of course syllabi and essays on the teaching of female studies, some of which deal with aspects of feminist criticism.[3] There is a growing number of organizations and publications through which feminist critics can exchange ideas: for example, Women's Caucus for the Modern Languages, International Institute of Women's Studies, *Women's Studies Newsletter, Women's Studies Quarterly,* and *Feminist Studies. Aphra* and *The Velvet Glove* identify themselves as feminist literary magazines and contain both original literature and literary criticism. Several of the contributors to *Female Studies* have written articles for other publications about women in literature or women writers. All of these articles use feminist criticism, whether they have defined it as such or not.

Feminist criticism has three distinct subdivisions, each with its own target. The first two are well defined and frequently practiced: (1) the analysis of the "image of women," nearly always as it appears in works by male authors; and (2) the examination of existing criticism of female authors. The third type still needs formulating, but it may become the crux of feminist criticism in the future. It is a "prescriptive" criticism that attempts to set standards for literature that is "good" from a feminist viewpoint. It is prescriptive in that it implies a need for new literature that meets its standards. It can guide authors who are writing literary works from a new feminist perspective, as well as those critics who are analyzing existing literature. Thus far it is directed almost exclusively toward female writers. Before defining this third type of criticism it is necessary to elaborate on the other two.

"Image of Women" Criticism

Of the twenty-seven courses on women in literature outlined in *Female Studies II*, five are entitled "Images of Women" or some such variation. Another five could easily bear that title. Nine more courses include, among other topics, a survey of female stereotypes in the works of male writers. The remaining eight deal primarily with female writers. The "Image of Women" approach was the earliest form of feminist criticism and is thus the most fully developed, having already produced its own hardcover texts.

The first of the recent works on female stereotypes in literature cannot actually be classified as feminist criticism: Leslie Fiedler's *Love and Death in the American Novel*, rev. ed. (New York: Stein and Day, 1966), employs a Jungian type of national character analysis that is scarcely compatible with feminism. Fiedler's own assumptions about female nature and his interpretation of the few works by women that he chooses to discuss call for a new feminist reading. Nevertheless, he does succeed in adding the Rose and the Lily, the classic female stereotypes in American literature, to the vocabulary of college freshmen.

Mary Ellmann's *Thinking about Women* (New York: Harcourt, Brace and World, 1968) moves beyond Fiedler's two types, finding an intricate mythological pattern of stereotyping in the works of American writers. According to Ellmann, the attributes that literature commonly ascribes to women are formlessness, passivity, instability (hysteria), confinement (narrowness, practicality), piety, materiality, spirituality, irrationality, compliancy, and incorrigibility (the shrew, the witch).

Of course, at this point, feminist critics and teachers take for granted the existence of female stereotypes in literature; the process of discovery is complete. One has only to say "Earth Mother," or "the Great American Bitch," and the features of the type immediately come to mind, along with one or two specific examples. Feminist criticism can now go on—to deal with the reasons behind this proliferation of female stereotypes and the lack of realistic women characters; to discuss the political uses of literary stereotypes; and to describe their effects on individual female consciousness.

Kate Millett's *Sexual Politics* (New York: Avon Books, 1971) offers the best synthesis so far of feminist literary and political analysis.

Millett sees the dehumanized examples of womanhood in the novels of Henry Miller and Norman Mailer not as anomalous fantasy figures, but rather as the *reductio ad absurdum* of the antifemale attitudes underlying the actual political relationship between the sexes. Whereas Fiedler sought nonliterary explanations for the stereotyping of women in American literature and posited an abnormal national psychology, Millett believes that Miller's, Mailer's, and D. H. Lawrence's portrayals of women reflect a "normal" state of affairs that is as old as patriarchy and not confined within national boundaries. Fiedler uses Freudian psychology as an exegetical method; Millett sees Freud as a culprit.

In *The Troublesome Helpmate* (Seattle: University of Washington Press, 1966) Katharine M. Rogers has chronicled a long tradition of literary misogyny. She says that the straightforward misogynistic pronouncements in early Christian and Classical Greek literature are forerunners of the fictional embodiments of misogynistic sentiment—the female stereotypes—in the modern novel. If misogyny is indeed an established literary convention, then an author might well follow it unconsciously, intending neither to impugn the characters of individual women nor to keep women as a class suppressed. Being male and not androgynous, men will naturally speak in terms of male experience. Virginia Woolf, the one early feminist critic whose writings have been revived and are read alongside modern critical works, would say that they write "with the male side of their brains."[4] Mental or psychic androgyny was, to Woolf, both an ideal and a possibility. American feminists hypothesize that it is the natural state to which we might return if the arbitrary constraints on male and female behavior, or "masculinity" and "femininity," were done away with.

Yet, a survey of the literature of the last century shows, if anything, a trend toward greater polarization. Feminist critics believe that novels by male authors are becoming more resolutely "masculine" and consequently even more misogynistic than before. The Rose, the dark-haired, sensuous, unsubmissive woman that Fiedler discovered in nineteenth-century American novels, became Hemingway's American Bitch. And Norman Mailer has made her still "bitchier."

For a while, the American Bitch coexisted with a redeeming female figure, the Mother-Savior (Faulkner's Dilsey in *The Sound and the Fury*, Steinbeck's Ma Joad in *The Grapes of Wrath*), but she has since evolved into Ken Kesey's Big Nurse.[5] To explain this trend, Dolores

Barracano Schmidt posits three reasons why a particular stereotype might appear in the works of several authors over a period of time: (1) "the character is derivative, the writers having used a common model"; (2) "the character is a product of social conditioning, an ideal or counter-ideal of the prevailing values of the society"; and (3) "the character is a symbolic fulfillment of the writers' needs, a mythical being invented to give solace in an otherwise terrifying situation." With respect to contemporary literary misogyny, Schmidt opts for the third reason, claiming that the terrifying situation in this case is the rise of feminist consciousness and its threats to male dominance.[6] Shulamith Firestone agrees: The novelists who make up "Virility, Inc.,"—her term for the hardboiled school—are reacting to the breakdown in rigid sex roles by creating a fantasy world in which women are subhuman.[7] This interpretation fits comfortably into Kate Millett's theory of sexual politics.

So far we have considered only obviously negative female stereotypes. The antithesis of the Rose and the Bitch is the Lily—the Fair-haired Maiden, the symbol of feminine purity, the woman-as-muse who flourished in European Romantic literature. What political significance does feminist criticism attach to this idealization of women? Does it imply that women were held in high regard in the society producing the literature? Here is Virginia Woolf's answer:

> Indeed, if woman had no existence save in the fiction written by men, one would imagine her a person of the utmost importance; very various; heroic and mean; splendid and sordid; infinitely beautiful and hideous in the extreme; as great as a man, some think even greater. But this is woman in fiction. In fact, as Professor Trevelyan points out, she was locked up, beaten and flung about the room.
>
> A very queer, composite being thus emerges. Imaginatively she is of the highest importance; practically she is completely insignificant. She pervades poetry from cover to cover; she is all but absent from history. She dominates the lives of kings and conquerors in fiction; in fact she was the slave of any boy whose parents forced a ring on her finger. Some of the most inspired words, some of the most profound thoughts in literature fall from her lips; in real life she could hardly read, could scarcely spell, and was the property of her husband.[8]

Contemporary American feminists pay scant attention to the idealization of women in earlier European literature, perhaps because of the urgent need to confront the current molders of American literary style, like Mailer, Bellow, Roth, and Updike. However, the idealized or "positive" female stereotype can, of course, be as antifeminist as the previously cited negative stereotypes. It obscures the actual social condition of women and induces them to seek consolation in myths rather than work for social change.

Once feminist critics have enumerated the female stereotypes in literature and discussed their political implications, how should they finally evaluate an antifeminist literary work? Shulamith Firestone first categorizes male writers according to motive: (1) "Male Protest Art"— this is "Virility, Inc.," which "self-consciously glorifies the male reality" as a reaction against feminism; (2) "The Male Angle"—this type "fails to achieve a comprehensive world view because it does not recognize that male reality is not Reality"; and (3) "(Individually Cultivated) Androgynous Mentality"—this type includes the films of Ingmar Bergman, which give "descriptions not of a liberated sexuality but of a still-unresolved conflict between the sexual and the human identity." According to Firestone, the writers in the first category are guilty; those in the second are ignorant. Of the third group, she warns, "great care would have to be taken that criticism be directed, not at the artists for their (accurate) portrayal of the imperfect reality, but at the grotesqueness of that reality itself as revealed by the art."[9]

Censors charged with reviewing pornography in the United States look for "redeeming social value" in sexually explicit works. Is it possible to find redeeming literary value in works that are socially repugnant? Apparently it is. Kate Millett has expressed her admiration for Lawrence's literary style. Annis Pratt writes: "It is difficult not to feel about Molly Bloom on her chamberpot what Eldridge Cleaver must feel about Jack Benny's Rochester, but a good critic will not withdraw her attention from a work which is resonant and craftsmanlike even if it is chauvinistic."[10] Dolores Barracano Schmidt writes:

> I do not mean in any way to denigrate the literary accomplishments of the authors referred to: Hemingway, Lewis, Fitzgerald are giants of twentieth-century fiction, here and abroad. I do

think, however, that we must reconsider our critical judgments and be particularly careful how we apply such sweeping critical terms as "realistic," "acute social observers," "universal in theme and values." They present a specifically *male* view, and in these particular cases, a threatened male view of their times.[11]

Lillian Robinson dissents, doubting whether sexist literature can have a literary value that is non-ideological: "I do not believe we have hitherto had objective standards by which to judge literary art, and the application of a feminist perspective will not mean adding ideology to a value-free discipline."[12]

If literary competence is a redeeming virtue, can it absolve sexist authors of social guilt? The verdict depends upon the ultimate political effect of their literary production. Do misogynistic writers abet the suppression of women? Do they do harm to individual female consciousness? Leslie Fiedler claims that stereotyping in American literature has created a serious dilemma for female readers:

> There are not, in fact, two orders of women, good and bad, nor is there even one which seems for a little while bad, only to prove in the end utterly unravished and pure. There are only two sets of expectations and a single imperfect kind of woman caught between them: only actual incomplete females, looking in vain for a satisfactory definition of their role in a land of artists who insist on treating them as goddesses or bitches. The dream role and the nightmare role alike deny the humanity of women, who, baffled, switch from playing out one to acting out the other.[13]

The use of female stereotypes as tools in sex-role socialization, the need for positive role-models, male authors' failure to provide realistic solutions to common female problems—these are the factors most frequently cited in discussing literature's social implications. Mary Anne Ferguson describes the emotional effect of misogynistic literature on her students:

> One of the problems in teaching "The Images of Women in Literature" is fighting the depression which builds up as the essentially negative reflection is documented in story after story; even women authors offer little hope as they show women wasting their lives tied to worthless men or driven to suicide by

the very awareness that such a course is trying to develop. One can try to substitute anger for depression, but the problem of channeling the anger constructively remains.[14]

The assignation of guilt, however, remains uncertain. Are authors morally obligated to use their talents in the cause of human rights? Are they culpable if they express their own prejudices or merely reflect prevailing social attitudes? Feminist critics have not resolved these questions.

The Case against "Phallic Criticism"

Feminist critics claim to have good cause for questioning scholarly objectivity and critical absolutism. Their dispute with established, reputedly non-ideological critics, most of whom are male, focuses on three allegations: (1) they fail to discuss female writers as writers, without regard to their sex; (2) they ignore many female writers altogether; and (3) they have a myopic tendency to make universal statements on the basis of male experience.

The allegedly biased critical treatment of female writers has been alternately termed "Phallic Criticism," "the Ovarian Theory of Literature," and "the Biological Put-down."[15] Mary Ellmann describes Phallic Criticism this way: "The discussion of women's books by men will arrive punctually at the point of preoccupation, which is the fact of femininity. Books by women are treated as though they themselves were women, and criticism embarks, at its happiest, upon an intellectual measuring of busts and hips."[16] Here is Kimberley Snow's definition of the same phenomenon:

> The Biological Put-down, in which women characters or authors are seen only in biological terms, is a perennial favorite in criticism. For example, one critic divides Faulkner's women into cows and bitches and another relates the poems of Emily Dickinson to her menstrual cycles. Male characters and authors, however, are not reduced to their biological functions or characteristics. No one divides Faulkner's men into studs or geldings, nor do they relate Carlyle's work to his indigestion, although the evidence is certainly there in both cases.[17]

Phallic Criticism, as described by feminist critics, assesses female writers in terms of their conformity to traditional notions about femininity. The resultant judgment is often equivocal. Anthony Burgess says that he cannot bear to read Jane Austen because she is too feminine. Yet he is equally critical of George Eliot for achieving a successful "male impersonation" and Ivy Compton-Burnett for writing "sexless" literature.[18] Some critics give backhanded praise to female authors who "transcend" their femininity, their words echoing Samuel Johnson's comparison of intellectual women to dancing dogs.[19] Critics like these are pleasantly surprised to encounter a woman "who writes like a man."[20] But others insist on it. Lionel Trilling, for example, dislikes Djuna Barnes's prose because it is not masculine enough.[21] Louis Auchincloss, writing about American female novelists as a group, says, "It is difficult to avoid the strident note, the shrill cry; it is hard to keep from becoming a crank."[22] He would not say the same of a male writer, for *strident*, *shrill*, and *crank* have feminine connotations.

A second exercise in Phallic Criticism is to admit grudgingly to the literary value of works by women, and then to deny that it is consciously attained. Sydney Dobell commented on the "involuntary art" of *Wuthering Heights*. Another nineteenth-century critic felt that women who wrote well did so "unawares."[23] Henry James likened Jane Austen to a spinster knitting absent-mindedly.[24]

Feminist critics note a double standard in literary criticism that relegates female writers to subcategory status.[25] "The working rule is simple, basic: There must always be two literatures like two public toilets, one for Men and one for Women."[26] Scholars are accustomed to dividing artistic products into "serious" and "popular" art. A cynic would say that a work of literature is "serious" if it appeals to the tastes of the academician making the classification, and "popular" if it is read by the non-academic public. Since there are so few women among those entitled to make such distinctions, it is not surprising that so few works by female authors are regarded as serious literature. Elaine Showalter, noting the near absence of female authors from college English syllabi, writes:

> Women students will therefore perceive that literature, as it is
> selected to be taught, confirms what everything else in the society

tells them: that the masculine viewpoint is considered normative, and the feminine viewpoint divergent. In the literary curriculum the woman writer is by definition "minor," recommended perhaps, but not required; likely to be a recluse, childless, or even mad, and yet lacking the phosphorescent glamor of the doomed male artist. In short, a woman studying English literature is also studying a different culture, to which she must bring the adaptability of the anthropologist.[27]

She goes on to say that female students are expected to internalize male values and to base their critical judgments upon them, deciding, as Virginia Woolf put it: "This is an important book . . . because it deals with war. This is an insignificant book because it deals with the feelings of women in a drawing-room."[28]

The cosmic terminology employed in literary criticism helps maintain the subcategory status of literature written by women. Only experiences encountered by male characters are called "universal" or basic to "the human condition." The "female experience" is peripheral to the central concern of literature—which is man's struggle with nature, God, fate, himself, and, not infrequently, woman. Woman is always "the Other."

These, then, are the primary faults that feminist critics find with standard literary criticism. What is the remedy? Is it enough to rid currently popular critical methods of sexist values? Feminist critics answer no on two counts. First, many, though by no means all, feminist critics dispute the New Criticism's claim to neutrality. Their dissatisfaction has found expression in a "ritual invective against the New Criticism"—its emphasis on form over content, its insistence on timelessness and universality, its probing for hidden significance. These, they say, are inapplicable to much of the literature written by women. For women like George Eliot and the Brontës, writing something other than sentimental novels was a rebellious act, and necessarily ideological and time-bound.[29] To understand a female author—or character— completely, the critic must take into account the social and legal status of women in her society. Feminist criticism is ultimately cultural criticism.

Second, nonsexist criticism will not correct the distortions that have already resulted from the application of a double standard. There is evidence showing that critical expectations have affected the style adopted by female writers.[30] Virginia Woolf believed that women either tried to write like men or wrote as men expected them to write: "In the one case they had created skillful parodies of the masculine style that would not, however, stand comparison with the originals; in the other case they had concocted an artificial feminine manner that did little more than flatter the bias of those who believed in the inferiority of women."[31] Perhaps the dictum that women are more prone to write "popular" literature is self-perpetuating. Because objective, "asexual" critical acclaim is virtually out of reach, women aim instead for commercial success. Another factor to consider is that novel-writing was one of the few ways in which nineteenth-century women could support themselves. There was a considerable market for sentimental literature, created by Samuel Richardson's *Pamela* and *Clarissa*, that has not survived the test of lasting value. Literary historians who survey this literature, without noting the economic condition of women at the time, might easily conclude that sentimentality is a natural trait in female writers, and continue to look for and expect it, even in contemporary literature.

Prescriptive Feminist Criticism

As a preface to the definition of Prescriptive Feminist Criticism, it would perhaps be helpful to take up some of the questions that have been left dangling in the summaries of the first two categories of feminist criticism. The answers to these questions will illuminate some of the assumptions underlying Prescriptive Criticism.

How do feminist critics deal with female writers who employ
female stereotypes in their works?

Feminist critics themselves have not completely abandoned the serious/popular dichotomy. Those critics who direct their attention to the deleterious images of women in "serious" literature can easily ignore the stereotypes created by female writers. Since female writers are seldom reviewed in major literary publications, included in literary histories, or read in college English classes, their readership is restricted from the outset; stereotypes in their works have little opportunity to affect social conditions or the self-images of individual females. The male literary paragons who are credited with capturing the essence of the human condition and depicting universal experience while they are stereotyping and even disparaging women, pose a greater threat.

There are feminists, though, who do study and criticize the effects of "popular" literature, evaluating soap operas, serial fiction, gothic romance, and semipornography or "pulp" fiction, areas in which women have achieved commercial success.[32] The stereotyping of women and the idealization of the traditional female role in popular culture were among the very first concerns of the new women's movement of the 1960s. The judgments Betty Friedan made in her critique of women's magazine literature in *The Feminine Mystique* (New York: Dell, 1963) are now widely accepted.

Rather than emphasize existing political transgressions, feminist critics prefer to concentrate on what female writers can do in their future works, urging them to forget literary convention when they create their female characters and to rely on their own subjective experience.[33] To win feminist acclaim, a literary work by a woman must first of all be *authentic*.[34] It need not be politically orthodox, nor even interpretive, so long as it is a realistic representation of "female experience," "feminine consciousness," or "female reality."[35]

*How does one decide whether a character
is realistic or stereotyped?*

One obvious check the reader might make on authenticity would be to compare the character's life with the author's. Of course, feminist criticism does not require fiction to be autobiographical; however, an author should combine personal recollection and subjective feelings with imagination and structural detail to create her female characters.

Women on Words and Images, a feminist task force in New Jersey, applied quantitative content analysis to a specific category of literature—elementary school readers—in order to judge the authenticity of the female characters depicted therein. One result of their work was to discover that only 3 working mothers appeared in 134 books, despite the fact that more than half of American women with children under 18 work outside the home.[36] Wendy Martin suggests comparing fictional heroines with historical figures such as Elizabeth Cady Stanton,

Amelia Earhart, and Margaret Fuller to determine whether fictional characterization is representative.[37]

While it is useful to compile statistical data on a collection of works from a limited time period to see how accurately they mirror female employment, educational attainment, marital status, birthrate, and the like, it is impossible to measure the authenticity of a single female protagonist's inner turmoil. The final test must be the subjective response of the female reader, who is herself familiar with "female reality." Does she recognize aspects of her own experience? The referent is, of course, dangerously narrow. Female reality is not monolithic, but has many nuances and variations. Nancy Hoffman explains why one of her class sessions on women writers was a failure:

> We *had*, in part, obliterated literature by stopping at the perennial Movement questions which *are* simply first questions: can I identify with this writer? does she relate to me? We should have answered, then moved on to ask, what does her experience mean if it is *not* mine? how do I define my own choice of consciousness except by comparison with alternative ones?[38]

How can feminist critics justify generalizing about
female experience and women writers, in light
of their objections to Phallic Criticism?

Feminists do not deny that women exhibit group characteristics. However, they do not accept the thesis that similarities in female behavior are biologically determined.[39] Critics who subscribe to "the Ovarian Theory of Literature" view women as a species with distinct, innate psychological characteristics (triviality, sentimentality) that are likely to affect literary style. Feminists interpret group characteristics as evidence that women constitute a caste, subject to special restrictive and limiting social influences. Elaine Showalter writes:

> Women writers should not be studied as a distinct group on the assumption that they write alike, or even display stylistic resemblances distinctively feminine. But women do have a special literary history susceptible to analysis, which includes such complex considerations as the economics of their relation to the literary marketplace; the effects of social and political changes in

women's status upon individuals, and the implications of stereotypes of the woman writer and restrictions of her artistic
autonomy.[40]

It may be necessary to reiterate that feminists *do* recognize the
obvious physical differences between men and women. Menstruation,
pregnancy (and the fear of it or desire for it), and childbirth are
important aspects of female experience and valid subjects for literary
expression. To counterbalance the use of women as sex objects in
contemporary literature, feminist critics seek subjective descriptions of
female sexuality.[41]

*Is there really a female culture? Do men and women actually
have different perceptions of reality?*

Firestone argues in *The Dialectic of Sex* that "the sex role system
divides human experience; men and women live in these different halves
of reality; and culture reflects this." Thus a novel that is true to
"female experience" and one that is true to "male experience" will
differ not only in style but also in subject matter. Firestone offers
"personal, subjective, emotional, descriptive vs. vigorous, spare, hard-
hitting, objective" as the dichotomy critics expect (p. 165).

Differing experiences result in differing values that cannot help but
affect literary tastes. Virginia Woolf complained that excessively masculine writers like Galsworthy and Kipling had no "suggestive power" for
their female readers.[42] Firestone interprets the popularity of love
stories among women as the "crude beginnings" of a demand for "a
'female' art to reinforce the female reality."[43] Ellen Harold says that
television comedy series with unconventional, rebellious, albeit flighty,
heroines who often outwit men are extremely popular among women.
She cites "I Love Lucy" and "Bewitched" as examples.[44]

Feminist critics offer no statistical data on differences in female and
male perception, but Showalter does relate a single observation. She
and her husband taught a seminar called "Sexual Themes in American
Novels in the 1960's." They noticed that the students responded
differently to the reading material, according to their sex: "Men, for
example, liked the lyrical rhapsodies on erotic themes in *Couples*, while
women found them slightly absurd; on the other hand, men found the

sexual descriptions in *The Group* deliberately mocking and sardonic, while women insisted that they were merely realistic."[45]

Joanna Russ posits a female subculture, arguing that women, too, perceive of culture as male and their own experience as peripheral:

> Culture is male. This does not mean that every man in Western (or Eastern) society can do exactly as he pleases, or that every man creates the culture *solus,* or that every man is luckier or more privileged than every woman. What it does mean (among other things) is that the society we live in, like all other historical societies, is a patriarchy. And patriarchies imagine or picture themselves from the male point of view. There is a female culture, but it is an underground, unofficial, minor culture, occupying a small corner of what we think of officially as possible human experience. Both men and *women* in our culture conceive the culture from a single point of view—the male.[46]

The major explanation, then, for the mounting interest in feminist criticism and the novels it recommends is the need for female readers to see their own experiences mirrored in literature. A frequent complaint is that few male authors, even those who are very sympathetic to women, have succeeded in portraying women with whom female readers can identify. "Women are estranged from their own experience and unable to perceive its shape and authenticity, in part because they do not see it mirrored and given resonance by literature. Instead they are expected to identify as readers with a masculine experience and perspective, which is presented as the human one."[47]

Is there an archetypal female experience corresponding to or complementing the male archetype?

This question is seldom raised by feminist critics. Annis Pratt, who defines feminist criticism in terms of current critical method, proposed at a Modern Language Association workshop on Feminist Literature and Feminine Consciousness that feminists adopt an archetypal mode of criticism:

> New feminist critics . . . may notice that the heroines they study manifest interestingly parallel characteristics during their

psychic development. It is startling to realize that volumes have been written about the development of the male psyche as if it, in itself, defined the human soul. If there is a "myth of the hero" there must also be a "myth of the heroine," a female as well as a male *bildungsroman*, parallel, perhaps, but by no means identical.

The heroines of fiction (as well as of poetry and drama) can be described as passing through the immanent phases of adolescent naturism, sexual initiation, marriage and childbirth in a quest for a transcendence that is sometimes separatist, sometimes androgynous, and sometimes visionary. We will thus find it helpful to develop a fourth and *archetypal* mode of new feminist criticism which will describe the psycho-mythological development of the female individual in literature.[48]

She was rebutted by Lillian Robinson, who questioned whether any archetype—male or female—could be free of ethnocentrism.[49] Joyce Nower is concerned with archetypal feminine experiences that go "beyond the observable" and suggests that feminist criticism also determine the extent to which male archetypes apply to women.[50]

If feminists who question the innateness of masculine and feminine behavior are to be consistent, they must reject analyses via literature of "the human condition" that ignore the socialization process which has determined each character's condition. Any attempt to construe a *natural* female condition from literary evidence would likely fall victim to Freudian analysis, which feminists find inadequate and fallacious. An exploration of female nature agreeable to feminists requires new psychological, anthropological and sociological methods, free of sexist bias, as well as a new literary criticism. Feminist critics may posit a female archetype, but any immediately forthcoming definition of it would surely be premature. Virginia Woolf wrote, in "Professions for Women": "What is a woman? I assure you, I do not know . . . I do not believe that anybody can know until she has expressed herself in all the arts and professions open to human skill."[51]

Are feminist critics concerned about style and aesthetic form?

The British feminist writers of the 1920s were closely allied with the experimentalists. Dorothy Richardson and May Sinclair developed stream-of-consciousness as a technique for exploring feminine consciousness.[52] Before the current revival of *A Room of One's Own* and *Three Guineas*, Virginia Woolf was better known as a member of the Bloomsbury group than as a feminist.[53]

Current American feminist critics speak of well-written books, but they have not yet established standards for good writing. Likewise, they say little about stylistic experimentation. Only Kate Millett, who is an artist as well as a critic, has appealed explicitly for new forms: "And if, indeed, we are saying something new, it does seem to me we ought to say it in new ways."[54] She proposes the flowing verbal monologue or dialogue as a suitable form for feminist art, taking advantage of women's flair for oral communication, and has used this form herself in her movie *Three Lives* (New York: Women's Liberation Cinema Company and Impact Films, 1971) and in a short work transcribed from tape called "Prostitution: A Quartet for Female Voices." In her Introduction to the latter, she speaks of the political role this form has played already in consciousness-raising sessions:

> When the prestigious intellectual and artistic media . . . are in the hands of those who govern, those out of power must settle for talk. One observes, for instance, a quite fantastic verbal ability in blacks. But women's talk has always been deliberately trivialized. And yet over the past five years, years I have spent in the women's movement, I have experienced a great change in such talk. There is a new cogency and direction, a clarity and rising consciousness in the speech of women now [p. 21].

The feminist playwright Myrna Lamb has invented a distinctive dramatic form: an intense, compact one-act play that relies on audience recognition of familiar, almost ritualistic experiences.

> She spares us the slow torture of a two-hour reenactment of our habitual follies and in return asks that we follow her fast, deft strokes carefully . . . . since we've all been through this routine so many times before, close attention will reveal that the labyrinth of her experience is more startlingly familiar to us than we might initially have thought.[55]

Ellen Morgan finds currently popular literary forms insufficient for expressing the political aspects of female experience, and she expects that "recastings" of three old forms—the *bildungsroman,* the historical novel, and the propaganda novel—will become the major feminist literary vehicles.

Neither the psychological nor the sociological novel is a form adequate to express the neo-feminist conception of woman, for she is not only a psyche, but a political being; not only a product and victim of her culture, but also a personal being who transcends it. The stream-of-consciousness novel, with its tendency to equate reality and value with consciousness cannot sufficiently express her experience, which is political and social as well as personal and psychological.[56]

Can feminists establish themselves as objective
literary critics, given their political orientation?

The opponents of Phallic Criticism doubt whether any form of criticism can be truly objective; methods that appear to be non-ideological are actually supporting the status quo.[57] Nancy Hoffman thinks it not only impossible, but even undesirable, to create a feminist criticism that is totally objective. Her classroom method integrates objective distance and emotional involvement.[58] Feminist critics recognize that theirs is a specialized, highly political type of analysis, only one of many to which literature might be subjected. There are, however, varying opinions about feminist criticism's place in the spectrum that ranges between ivory tower academism and political activism. Lillian Robinson speaks from the political end:

> Some people are trying to make an honest woman out of the feminist critic, to claim that every "worthwhile" department should stock one. I am not terribly interested in whether feminism becomes a respectable part of academic criticism; I am very much concerned that feminist critics become a useful part of the women's movement.[59]

Because of its origin in the women's liberation movement, feminist criticism values literature that is of some use to the movement. Prescriptive Criticism, then, is best defined in terms of the ways in which literature can serve the cause of liberation. To earn feminist approval, literature must perform one or more of the following functions: (1) serve as a forum for women; (2) help to achieve cultural androgyny; (3) provide role-models; (4) promote sisterhood; and (5) augment consciousness-raising. I would like to discuss these functions one by one.

In order to be useful as a *forum*, literature must allow forthright and honest self-expression, writing which is not constrained by pre-existing standards that may be alien to female culture. Virginia Woolf's first directive to female writers was: "Above all, you must illumine your own soul with its profundities and its shallows, and its vanities and its generosities, and say what your beauty means to you or your plainness." She regretted that the female author of the nineteenth century wrote with "a mind which was slightly pulled from the straight, and made to alter its clear vision in deference to external authority."[60] Ellen Morgan renews Woolf's advice: "Feminist criticism should, I believe, encourage an art true to women's experience and not filtered through a male perspective or constricted to fit male standards."[61] On the other hand, authors should not feel obligated to offer an exact representation of their own lives, but rather "the fictional myths *growing out of their lives* and told by themselves for themselves."[62] The arts must help people understand what female experience is, "what it's like, what you think, how it operates. What it feels like to be us."[63] Before literature can begin to perform the other functions, however, it must express female experience authentically, in all its variety. The emphasis on variety is apparent in the course syllabi in the *Female Studies* series. The works selected represent various ages, classes, and races of women. Tillie Olsen's "Women: A List Out of Which to Read," which appears in cumulative fashion in the *Women's Studies Newsletter* (Old Westbury, New York: The Feminist Press), is an example of a growing tendency on the part of feminist critics and teachers to seek out materials that will compass the totality of the female life experience.

Once literature begins to serve as a forum, illuminating female experience, it can assist in humanizing and equilibrating the culture's value system, which has historically served predominantly male interests.

That is, it can help to bring about *cultural androgyny*. Carolyn Heilbrun has reintroduced Woolf's "androgyny" into the vocabulary of literary criticism in her book *Toward a Recognition of Androgyny* (New York: Alfred A. Knopf, 1973).[64] Other feminist critics agree that a "female impulse" in literature is necessary for the achievement of cultural androgyny. Firestone expresses it succinctly: The "development of 'female' art . . . is progressive: an exploration of strictly female reality is a necessary step to correct the warp in a sexually biased culture. It is only after we have integrated the dark side of the moon into our world view that we can begin to talk seriously of universal culture."[65] Of course, a pluralistic society like the one that exists in the United States must also draw on the experiences of its ethnic and regional groups if it is to be truly balanced.

Feminists often emphasize that they are not simply seeking more room for women in the present social order. They want a new social order founded on "humanistic" values, some of which are traditionally "female" and not respected in contemporary society. Those traditionally "male" values that feminists believe harmful to the common good— excessive competition, for example—would be de-emphasized. Therefore, a female literary personage with "masculine" characteristics does not necessarily meet with feminist approval. Ellen Harold, writing about Emma Peel, the heroine of "The Avengers," a British television series shown in the United States, comments: "What is truly sad is that, though she is equal to a man and superior to most men, the measure of her competence is a strictly *macho* one—her capacity for violence. As an attempt at an emancipated woman she leaves something to be desired, for both men and women need new standards against which to measure themselves."[66]

A literary work should provide *role-models*, instill a positive sense of feminine identity by portraying women who are "self-actualizing, whose identities are not dependent on men."[67] This function is particularly crucial in children's literature. In *Dick and Jane as Victims,* Women on Words and Images find fault with elementary school readers for reserving active mastery skills for boys—that is, creativity, ingenuity, adventurousness, curiosity, perseverance, bravery, autonomy—and describing girls as passive, docile, dependent, incompetent, and self-effacing. Adult women who are re-examining their lives may also depend on literature to introduce new possibilities and to help them evaluate the alternatives open to them. "We cannot live in a certain way, we cannot see ourselves as the people we wish to be, until we perceive the wished-for life and self in our imaginations."[68] To compensate for the dearth of satisfactory fictional role-models, feminist teachers are enlarging the definition of literature to include biography, autobiography, and memoirs. The syllabus for the Women's Biography Course offered at California State University in Sonoma illustrates the urgency of the search for role-models.[69]

It is important to note here that although female readers need literary models to emulate, characters should not be idealized beyond plausibility. The demand for authenticity supercedes all other requirements. Mary Anne Ferguson assigns works like Tillie Olsen's *Tell Me a Riddle* and Willa Cather's *My Antonia* to help her students "realize that liberation involves hard choices; that it begins and ends with the self; that self-knowledge depends upon contact with the real world."[70]

Literature should show women involved in activities that are not traditionally "feminine," to speed the dissolution of rigid sex roles. It is not enough, however, to simply place a female character in a new occupation, with no corresponding change in her personality and behavior. Marion Meade describes the effects of the women's liberation movement on television heroines: although a few series feature female doctors or lawyers or television producers, the women's behavior and their relationships with men follow the familiar stereotyped pattern. They are caricatures, not realistic women, she says.[71]

The feminist movement in America is seeking to create a feeling of *sisterhood*, a new sense of community among women, in order to overcome group self-hatred, the animosity that many women feel for others of their sex as a result of isolation, competition for male attention, and belief in female inferiority. Virginia Woolf noticed the dearth of gratifying woman-to-woman relationships in literature:

> "Chloe liked Olivia," I read. And then it struck me how immense a change was there. Chloe liked Olivia perhaps for the first time in literature. Cleopatra did not like Octavia. And how completely *Antony and Cleopatra* would have been altered had she done so! . . . All these relationships between women, I

thought, rapidly recalling the splendid gallery of fictitious women, are too simple. So much has been left out, unattempted.[72]

In addition to testing new female-female (and female-male) relationships, a literary work can serve the cause of sisterhood by recounting experiences that the reader can identify as her own, experiences that are, perhaps, shared by many women. She will feel a common bond with the author and other readers who have similar reactions to the book. This is vital for adolescent readers, says Susan Koppelman Cornillon:

> We are all aware of the agony of adolescence in our culture, the evasive fumblings as we attempt to communicate about our fears and our needs and our anxieties without actually ever mentioning to anyone what they really are: the creation of elaborate private symbologies that enable us to grieve about our pimples, our sexual fantasies, our masturbation, the strange changes happening to our bodies. But boys outgrow this secretiveness soon—because there is a vast wealth of literature for them to stumble on, both great and popular, classical and contemporary, pious and lewd, that assures them that, indeed, they are normal. Or even better, their suffering is portrayed as a prerequisite for maturity, if not a prelude to greatness.[73]

Literature might also enable a reader to empathize with women whose subjective accounts of female reality differ from her own.

> Loving someone is wanting to know them. Insofar as we are able to learn and know of each other, we can acknowledge, and even in part assimilate into our own imaginative life, the thousand differences that have always been used as wedges to drive us apart. So that the experience of all women everywhere becomes, in a sense, our communal property, a heritage we bestow upon each other, the knowledge of what it has meant to be female, a woman in this man's world.[74]

In order to augment *consciousness-raising*, literature should provide realistic insights into female personality development, self-perception, interpersonal relationships, and other "private" or "internal" consequences of sexism. The reader can then note recurring problems and generalize from them with the aid of factual information about the status of women from other sources.[75] Feminist critics are far more concerned with exposing these private effects than with raising concrete issues, such as job discrimination and lack of child care facilities. In this age of mass communications, public forums, and official investigative committees, fiction is no longer the most effective means of arousing concern about measurable social problems. That is not to say that concrete political issues have no place in feminist-approved literature. But their presence must be consistent with the demands for authenticity and subjectivity prerequisite to an effective integration of the personal and the political. In disparaging didactic feminist poetry, Erica Jong noted, "We all claim to believe that political oppression and personal feelings are related, and yet a great deal of the self-consciously polemical poetry that has come out of the Women's Movement reads like a generalized rant and it lacks any sort of psychological grounding. The poet has not really looked into herself and told it true. She has been content to echo simplistic slogans."[76] Likewise, a fictional account of job discrimination that covers only the material consequences will not suffice. If the protagonist is, indeed, fully characterized, we will also see the private or psychic effects of discrimination. Ellen Morgan values a subtle rendering of both types of problems in which "neo-feminist consciousness informs the novel as light informs a painting, rather than appearing as subject matter."[77]

There is a precedent for this sort of personalized polemic in black literature. James Baldwin's novels are not single-issue tracts, but rather in-depth studies of individual examples of black humanity. Ralph Ellison's *Invisible Man* was successful not because it exposed conditions that were completely foreign to whites in America, but because it appealed to common, multiracial feelings of insignificance and alienation, showing how much more intense they are when institutionalized. Perhaps the difference between this and the muckraking and Socialist literatures of the early twentieth century is due to the fact that the victims have become the authors.[78]

Factual information about discrimination should be carefully integrated into a story with a larger focus, so that its presence seems natural. Joyce Nower warns, however, against condemning the author who merely translates position papers into fiction: "A woman artist who writes a lousy story on a woman active in the Movement, or involved in getting an abortion, should be accorded the respect of critical appraisal: a lousy writer but important in that she is trying to use new materials."[79] Ellen Morgan concurs: "The capacity to teach and to delight which some of this work has would suggest that critical standards which deny literary legitimacy and value to [propagandistic] writing may be inadequate tools for [its] evaluation."[80]

No feminist critic insists that a fictional work include political analysis.[81] The author need only describe the problems and offer some solutions, if the character herself can find them. The remaining tasks involved in consciousness-raising are left to the reader: to compare the problems encountered by female literary characters with her own, to explain similarities in terms of causes, and to decide on appropriate political action. Literature can thus augment the face-to-face consciousness-raising that is fundamental to the American women's liberation movement.

There is a potential conflict between the consciousness-raising function and the role-model function. A work that offers a thorough literary description of women's oppression may also feature a "heroine" who is thoroughly oppressed and therefore unlikely to be emulated by female readers. Erica Jong, for one, is dissatisfied with "all those so-called feminist novels in which women are depicted as helpless victims."[82] The ideal feminist fictional work is one that fulfills all five functions in equilibrium. Rather than being driven to mental breakdown or suicide or immobility, the heroines of new feminist fiction will somehow manage to resist destruction, perhaps with the support and confidence of other women. Their outlook and behavior will presage a new social order that integrates the best aspects of "female culture" with selected "male" values.

NOTES

1. *Redbook*, November 1972, pp. 199-221. See Mary Colwell, "Kate Chopin: Writer Unknown," *Women: A Journal of Liberation* 2(Fall 1970):10-11.

2. Florence Howe, "A Report on Women and the Profession," *College English* 32(May 1971):851.

3. *Female Studies I* (Pittsburgh: KNOW, 1970) was a completely independent project undertaken by Sheila Tobias. It includes only one literature course. The

other volumes in this series are: *Female Studies II*, ed. Florence Howe (1970); *Female Studies III*, ed. Florence Howe and Carol Ahlum (1971); *Female Studies IV: Teaching about Women*, ed. Elaine Showalter and Carol Ohmann (1972); and *Female Studies V: Proceedings of the Conference Women and Education: A Feminist Perspective*, ed. Rae Lee Siporin (1972). The Feminist Press, Old Westbury, New York, has published two additional volumes: *Female Studies VI: Closer to the Ground*, ed. Nancy Hoffman, Cynthia Secor, and Adrian Tinsley (1972); and *Female Studies VII: Going Strong—New Courses/New Programs*, ed. Deborah Silverton Rosenfelt (1973).

4. Virginia Woolf, *A Room of One's Own* (New York: Harcourt, Brace and World, 1929), p. 105.

5. Kimberley Snow, "Images of Women in American Literature," *Aphra* 2(Winter 1970):56-68.

6. Dolores Barracano Schmidt, "The Great American Bitch," *College English* 32(May 1971):900.

7. Shulamith Firestone, *The Dialectic of Sex: The Case for Feminist Revolution*, rev. ed. (New York: Bantam, 1971), pp. 167-69.

8. Woolf, *A Room of One's Own*, pp. 45-46.

9. Firestone, *Dialectic of Sex*, pp. 167-69.

10. Annis Pratt, "The New Feminist Criticism," *College English* 32(May 1971):877.

11. Schmidt, "The Great American Bitch," p. 905.

12. Lillian Robinson, "Dwelling in Decencies," *College English* 32(May 1971):888.

13. Leslie Fiedler, *Love and Death in the American Novel*, rev. ed. (New York: Stein and Day, 1966), p. 314.

14. Quoted by Elaine Showalter in "Introduction: Teaching about Women, 1971," *Female Studies IV*, ed. Showalter and Ohmann, pp. ix-x.

15. Respectively, by Mary Ellmann in *Thinking about Women* (New York: Harcourt, Brace and World, 1968); by Cynthia Ozick in "Women and Creativity: The Demise of the Dancing Dog," *Woman in Sexist Society: Studies in Power and Powerlessness*, ed. Vivian Gornick and Barbara K. Moran (New York: Basic Books, 1971), pp. 307-22; and by Snow, in "Images of Women in American Literature."

16. Ellmann, *Thinking about Women*, p. 29.

17. Snow, "Images of Women in American Literature," p. 67.

18. Ellmann, *Thinking about Women*, p. 40.

19. Note Ozick's subtitle, "The Demise of the Dancing Dog," in note 15 above.

20. Ellmann, *Thinking about Women*, p. 31.

21. Lionel Trilling, *The Liberal Imagination: Essays on Literature and Society* (Garden City, New York: Anchor Books of Doubleday, 1953), p. 263.

22. Louis Auchincloss, *Pioneers and Caretakers: A Study of Nine American Women Novelists* (Minneapolis: University of Minnesota Press, 1965), p. 4.

23. Carol Ohmann, "Emily Brontë in the Hands of Male Critics," *College English* 32 (May 1971):909.

24. Wayne C. Booth, *The Rhetoric of Fiction* (Chicago: University of Chicago Press, 1961), pp. 243-44.

25. Carol Ohmann has compiled evidence of different critical standards for male and female writers. See "Emily Brontë in the Hands of Male Critics," pp. 906-13, in which she gives an account of the change in critical evaluations of

Wuthering Heights after it was revealed that Ellis Bell was actually Emily Brontë.
26. Ellmann, *Thinking about Women*, p. 33.
27. Elaine Showalter, "Women and the Literary Curriculum," *College English* 32(May 1971):856.
28. Woolf, *A Room of One's Own*, p. 77. See also Charlotte Perkins Gilman's critique of male literary criticism in *The Man-Made World, or Our Androcentiic Culture* (New York: Charlton, 1911), chapter 5.
29. Robinson, "Dwelling in Decencies," p. 888.
30. Elaine Showalter, "Women Writers and the Double Standard," *Woman in Sexist Society*, ed. Gornick and Moran, pp. 323-43.
31. Herbert Marder, *Feminism and Art: A Study of Virginia Woolf* (Chicago: University of Chicago Press, 1968), p. 121.
32. Susan Koppelman Cornillon of the Center for the Study of Popular Culture at Bowling Green University in Bowling Green, Ohio, has done much work in this area.
33. Millett, *Sexual Politics*, p. 139.
34. Ibid.; Firestone, *Dialectic of Sex*, p.157; Showalter, "Women and the Literary Curriculum," p. 856; Snow, "Images of Women in American Literature," p. 68; Barbara Alson Wasserman, *The Bold New Women*, rev. ed. (Greenwich, Connecticut: Fawcett Publications, 1970), p. 9; and Ellen Morgan, Princeton Junction, New Jersey, to author, February 13, 1972. [See also Holly's essay in this collection. Ed.]
35. So called, respectively, by Kate Millett in "Notes on the Making of *Three Lives*," mimeographed (New York, 1971), p. 2; by Sylvia Robinson Corrigan in "Art and Marriage," *Aphra* 2(Winter 1970):12; and Sydney Kaplan in " 'Featureless Freedom' or Ironic Submission: Dorothy Richardson and May Sinclair," *College English* 32(May 1971):914; and by Firestone in *Dialectic of Sex*, p. 167.
36. Women on Words and Images, *Dick and Jane as Victims: Sex Stereotyping in Children's Readers,* self-published (Princeton, New Jersey, 1972). A similar method was used by Ruth Ingles in 1938 to determine whether magazine short stories reflect society or operate as a social control. She surveyed the fictional heroines in *The Saturday Evening Post* in "An Objective Approach to the Relationship between Literature and Society," *American Sociological Review* 3(August 1938):526-33.
37. Wendy Martin, "The Feminine Mystique in American Fiction," *Female Studies II*, ed. Howe, p. 33.
38. Nancy Hoffman, "A Class of Our Own," *Female Studies IV*, ed. Showalter and Ohmann, p. 16. See also Nancy Burr Evans, "The Value and Peril for Women of Reading Women Writers," *Images of Women in Fiction: Feminist Perspectives*, ed. Susan Koppelman Cornillon (Bowling Green, Ohio: Bowling Green University Popular Press, 1972).
39. Naomi Weisstein, " 'Kinder, Kuche, Kirche' as Scientific Law: Psychology Constructs the Female," *Sisterhood Is Powerful*, ed. Robin Morgan (New York: Vintage, 1970), pp. 205-19; and Phyllis Chesler, "Men Drive Women Crazy," *Psychology Today*, July 1971, pp. 18-27, 97-99.
40. Showalter, "Women and the Literary Curriculum," pp. 858-59.
41. Ibid., p. 859; idem, "Women Writers and the Double Standard," p. 343; Wasserman, *The Bold New Women*, p. 10; and Joyce Nower, Publications Coordinator, Center for Women's Studies and Services, San Diego, to author, March 7, 1972.

42. Woolf, *A Room of One's Own*, p. 106.
43. Firestone, *Dialectic of Sex*, p. 167.
44. Ellen Harold, "A Look at Some Old Favorites," *Aphra* 2(Spring 1971):38-45.
45. Showalter, "Women and the Literary Curriculum," p. 859.
46. Joanna Russ, "What Can a Heroine Do? or Why Women Can't Write," *Images of Women in Fiction*, ed. Koppelman Cornillon, p. 4.
47. Showalter, "Women and the Literary Curriculum," p. 856.
48. Pratt, "The New Feminist Criticism," pp. 876-77.
49. Robinson, "Dwelling in Decencies," p. 884.
50. Joyce Nower to author, March 7, 1972.
51. Quoted by Corrigan in "Art and Marriage," p. 14.
52. Kaplan, " 'Featureless Freedom' or Ironic Submission," p. 914.
53. Herbert Marder tries to correct this imbalance by stressing the interdependence of Woolf's art and feminism in *Feminism and Art: A Study of Virginia Woolf*. The recent publication of three books on Woolf has set off a reevaluation of her work: Quentin Bell, *Virginia Woolf: A Biography* (New York: Harcourt Brace Jovanovich, 1972); Joan Russell Noble, *Recollections of Virginia Woolf* (New York: William Morrow, 1972); and Nancy Topping Bazin, *Virginia Woolf and the Androgynous Vision* (New Brunswick, New Jersey: Rutgers University Press, 1972). See also Margaret Drabble, "How Not To Be Afraid of Virginia Woolf," *Ms.*, November 1972, pp. 68-70, 72, 121.
54. Kate Millett, "Introduction" to "Prostitution: A Quartet for Female Voices," *Woman in Sexist Society*, ed. Gornick and Moran, p. 21.
55. Anselma Dell'Olio, "Introduction" to Myrna Lamb, "Two Plays on Love and Marriage," *Woman in Sexist Society*, ed. Gornick and Moran, p. 5.
56. Ellen Morgan, "Humanbecoming: Form and Focus in the Neo-Feminist Novel," *Images of Women in Fiction*, ed. Koppelman Cornillon, p. 183.
57. Lillian Robinson and Lise Vogel, "Modernism and History," *Images of Women in Fiction*, ed. Koppelman Cornillon, pp. 278-305; and Fraya Katz-Stoker, "The Other Criticism: Feminism vs. Formalism," ibid., pp. 313-25.
58. Hoffman, "A Class of Our Own," pp. 14-27.
59. Robinson, "Dwelling in Decencies," p. 889.
60. Woolf, *A Room of One's Own*, pp. 93, 77.
61. Ellen Morgan to author, February 13, 1972.
62. Russ, "What Can a Heroine Do?" p. 19.
63. Millett, "Notes on the Making of *Three Lives*," p. 2.
64. See also Carolyn Heilbrun, "The Masculine Wilderness of the American Novel," *Saturday Review*, January 29, 1972, pp. 41-44.
65. Firestone, *Dialectic of Sex*, p. 167.
66. Harold, "A Look at Some Old Favorites," pp. 44-45.
67. Martin, "The Feminine Mystique in American Fiction," p. 33.
68. Michele Murray, "Introduction" to *A House of Good Proportion, Images of Women in Literature*, ed. Murray (New York: Simon and Schuster, 1973), p. 19.
69. *Female Studies VII*, ed. Rosenfelt, pp. 82-85.
70. Quoted in Showalter, "Introduction: Teaching about Women, 1971," p. x.
71. Marion Meade, "On the Trail of the Liberated TV Heroine," *Aphra* 2(Spring 1971):30-34.

72. Woolf, *A Room of One's Own*, p. 86.
73. Susan Koppelman Cornillon, "The Fiction of Fiction," *Images of Women in Fiction*, ed. Koppelman Cornillon, p. 115.
74. Millett, "Introduction" to "Prostitution: A Quartet," p. 23. See also Hoffman, "A Class of Our Own."
75. See Morgan's critique of Alix Kates Schulman, *Memoirs of an Ex-Prom Queen* (New York: Alfred A. Knopf, 1972) in "Humanbecoming," pp. 197-204.
76. Erica Jong, "Visionary Anger" (a review of Adrienne Rich, *Diving Into the Wreck*) *Ms.*, July 1973, p. 31.
77. Morgan, "Humanbecoming," p. 197.
78. For a discussion of this earlier literature see Walter B. Rideout, *The Radical Novel in the United States, 1900-1954: Some Interrelations of Literature and Society* (Cambridge: Harvard University Press, 1956).
79. Joyce Nower to author, March 7, 1972.
80. Morgan, "Humanbecoming," p. 187.
81. With the possible exception of Kate Millett. In *Sexual Politics*, p. 139, she criticizes Virginia Woolf for not explaining the causes of Rhoda's suicidal misery in *The Waves*, but in "Notes on the Making of *Three Lives*," written two years later, she says that she would now rather *express* female experience than analyze it.
82. Jong, "Visionary Anger," p. 34.

SUBJECTIVITIES: A THEORY OF
THE CRITICAL PROCESS

Dorin Schumacher

Can the literary critic be compared to the poet, responding creatively, intuitively, subjectively to the written word as the poet responds creatively and individually to the world of human experience? Does the critic interpret an artist's work in the same way that the artist has interpreted experience, reaching truth through intuitive, untraceable leaps of consciousness? Or is the literary critic a kind of scientist, reaching for truth by following a series of demonstrable, verifiable steps, using a scientific method or process?

The old subjectivity vs. objectivity or critic-as-artist-or-scientist debate has special significance for the theoretician of feminist criticism; for her, the question is not only academic, but political as well, and her definition will court special risks whichever side of the issue it seems to favor. If she defines feminist criticism as objective and scientific, a valid, verifiable intellectual method that anyone can perform, whether male or female, then the definition precludes not only the critic-as-poet approach, but also the utilitarian objectives of those who seek to change the academic establishment and its thinking, especially with regard to sex roles. If she defines feminist criticism as creative and intuitive, privileged as art, then the method becomes vulnerable to the

This discussion is based on the results of linguistic research carried out with members of the Machine Intelligence Group of the Graduate School of Business, School of Medicine, University of Pittsburgh. A report of this work proposing use of the computer as a tool to discover the problem-solving process of criticism was presented in Schumacher's paper, "Feminization of the Theatrical Universe of Jean Giraudoux: A Computer Analysis," Computers and Literature Section, MMLA Convention, November 1972. The discussion of Giraudoux's text is based upon her dissertation, "Imagery of Theatricality in the Theatre of Jean Giraudoux," University of Pittsburgh, 1971.

prejudices of stereotypic thinking about "the feminine" and can be dismissed by much of the academic establishment. Feminist critics may find themselves charged with the inability to be analytical, to be objective, or to think critically. While the male critic may be free to claim the role of critic-as-artist, the female critic runs different professional risks if she chooses intuition and private experience as critical method and defense.

So the theoretician must steer a delicate philosophical course between the Scylla of "masculine" objective dryness and the Charybdis of "feminine" poetic delirium. Yet the politics of shipwreck can be avoided, I think, if we can construct a theory of feminist criticism within the framework of a general theory of the critical process that is neither purely objective nor purely intuitive; in that way, its processes can be examined beside, compared with, and contrasted to other branches of criticism with some degree of dispassionate distance.

Literary criticism is scientific in the sense that it is an orderly linguistic modeling process whose rules can be understood, stated, and are subject to verification. The syntax and semantics of a given text assume meaning according to an idea, or interpretive model, which the critic applies to the text as a whole. Criticism can thus be defined as the transformation of an idea into semantic and syntactic correlates.

Literary criticism is also an artistic process in the sense that through it, the critic actually creates the meaning of a text. Criticism is not a reactive reading for literal understanding, but an active, interpretive, assertive reading that itself *creates* meaning. In a simple reading for understanding, it is enough to find an obvious meaning that is logically or experientially adequate. The literary critic, however, selects and defines an idea, or interpretive model, and then uses it to seek out extended meanings for the words of the text as they relate to that model. Thus, since the basic semantic and syntactic data of a text are manipulated by the critic, the meaning s/he produces is individual; but the work is accomplished according to specific rules, and always within the framework dictated by the selected idea.

This theory of the critical process can be illustrated by taking a sentence from Jean Giraudoux's play, *Pour Lucrèce,* and then defining its syntactic and semantic data according to different interpretive models. The sentence reads as follows: "Elle est entrée dans un palace d'où elle est vue de l'univers, dont les murs, les plafonds sont tendus de mille miroirs qui renvoient ses moindres gestes, dont la résonance est telle que jusqu'à ses soupirs éclatent." [She has entered a palace from which she is seen by the universe, whose walls, whose ceilings are hung with a thousand mirrors reflecting her slightest gestures, whose resonance is such that even her sighs thunder.] [1]

A simple reading of this would yield a literal interpretation: a woman has actually entered a palace. However, the critic can completely change the significance, or meanings, of the semantic and syntactic data simply by applying the idea of *theatricalism* to the text. First the critic would break *theatricalism* into component parts— "actor," "stage," "audience," "director," "costume," "lighting," "gesture," "make-up,"—and assign each part a general syntactic and/or semantic correlate. (For example, "actor" would probably govern proper names, personal pronouns, nouns of person; "stage," the nouns of location, physical place; "audience," the words indicating watchers, listeners.) Then the critic would search the text for syntactic and semantic matches. For example, "Elle est entrée dans un palace d'où elle est vue de l'univers," would become "Actor makes stage entrance onto stage where actor is seen by audience." In this way, the component parts of the idea *theatricalism* dictate the new meanings that the critic assigns to the words in the text. A schematic diagram of the process might look like this:

Theatricalism → ACTOR	→ proper noun, person →	SHE	→ SHE = ACTOR
STAGE	→ place	→ PALACE	→ PALACE = STAGE
AUDIENCE →	persons watching	→ UNIVERSE →	UNIVERSE = AUDIENCE

The same critic can, of course, create different meanings, or different critics can create alternate meanings in a text by applying different ideas to it. The literal denotation of the word "palace," for example, is simply the residence of a king. However, if the critic were seeking to determine Giraudoux's or his character's idea of *love*, and applied that model to the text, then "palace" would carry connotations of romance, courtly love, aristocratic love games, any and all extended meanings that could be derived from historical and literary ideas of love associated with a palace. If the critic applied the idea of *self*, then "palace" could become the place of the mind, or consciousness itself.

In the same way, the critic would interpret the syntax of the text. A literal reading of the verb "has entered," for example, yields simply the physical act of going into one place from another; but when the idea of *love* is applied to the text, "has entered" suggests a voluntary change of emotion or experience; when *self* is applied, it becomes the psychological act of going from one state of consciousness to another. Apply *theatricalism* and, as we have seen above, "has entered" becomes the act of making an entrance onto a stage.

Once applied then, the critic's idea, or model, determines all word associations and connotations used to interpret the text; and ultimately, the "meaning" so created exists as a kind of critical "fact."

Using the process described above, a critic may consciously or unconsciously apply a sex-linked idea to a text, and the meaning and values of the words in the text will be affected accordingly. Biological and cultural definitions of male and female can thus be extended intellectually, resulting in a sex-linked interpretation of the text to which they are applied. There are two approaches to sex-linked criticism, of course, here called "masculinist" and "feminist." Both may assume that male and female exhibit group characteristics that are biologically determined or socially defined or both, and both may make dichotomous, value-associated assumptions about the two sexes. Some of the dichotomous assumptions that might be used in a sex-linked interpretive model are passive-active, body-mind, feeling-intellect, internal-external, superior-inferior. One possible sex-linked idea or model, and the one that will be analyzed in detail in this essay, is based upon the self-other dichotomy, discussed in Simone de Beauvoir's feminist criticism in *The Second Sex* (New York: Alfred A. Knopf, 1953).[2] It is based upon the assumption that one sex is normative, or *self*, and the other deviant, or *other*. To the masculinist critic applying this model, male would be self and female other; to the feminist critic applying this model, female would be self and male other.

In either case, the rules of the critical process are the same. First the critic would break the idea down into its component parts, *selfness* yielding, for example, "internality," "activity," "consciousness," and "will"; *otherness*, "externality," "passivity," "physicality." Next, the critic would find syntactic and semantic correlates for these parts: the components of *selfness* governing such parts of speech as subjects, the active voice, and verbs and nouns of mental activity (thinking, knowing, perceiving, seeing, feeling); the components of *otherness* governing objects, the passive voice, and verbs and nouns of physical attributes and movements. Now, applying *self-other* to the same Giraudoux sentence, the critic would create the following transformation: "She (self/ other) has entered a palace where she (other) is seen by the universe (self) whose walls, whose ceilings are hung with a thousand mirrors (self) that reflect her (other) slightest gestures, whose resonance is such that even her (self) sighs thunder." The masculinist and the feminist critic would both arrive at the same text transformation, and both would agree that in this sentence *selfness* resides mostly outside the woman, for "she is seen by the universe," and in "mirrors"; she is perceived by something external; she is physically reflected. She has the primarily physical existence of *otherness:* "She has entered," "she is seen," "gestures," "sighs." She is acted upon physically by selves outside of her. She is other.

For the masculinist critic, since man is self and woman is other, the passage as it has been interpreted is adequate and satisfies the masculinist model for truth about woman. She is other, she is body; consciousness resides outside of her. It is probably safe to say that most of literature and literary criticism fits this masculinist model for truth.

For the feminist critic, the text must be further transformed since feminist criticism's idea of male-female says that woman is self and man is other. The feminist critic assumes a self in woman and interprets the data of the text as though a self exists. That is, if woman as self is not found in the text, the critic hypothesizes the self and explains its absence from the text. In this case, the woman's self may be read as having been voluntarily given up ("has entered"); or repressed ("universe," "mirrors," "resonance"); as being sick and weak ("least gestures," "sighs"); or trapped ("palace"); or turned in upon itself ("mirrors," "resonance"). The critic may posit cause for the self's absence in another character's actions, in the writer's perceptions, or in cultural attitudes. If the application of the *self-other* idea to the text produced a meaning where woman were self and man other, then the feminist model for truth about woman would be satisfied. In the same way, the masculinist critic would then have to hypothesize the existence of a male self and explain its absence in some way.

A significant difference in the problems facing the masculinist critic and the feminist critic becomes evident when the critic desires to apply a supportive critical idea to the text, a universal concept that can be related to the masculinist or the feminist meaning. The masculinist critic has a wide selection of critical ideas from which to choose, found in those philosophies that have a male-female biological model, such as Freudian, Jungian, or Christian, or in other constructs that include male and female social definitions, such as political, economic, or historical theory. These philosophies include in themselves the masculinist idea of man as self, or normative, and woman as other, or deviant. Moreover, they would seem to lend strength and intellectual weight to the masculinist interpretation by force of their respectability.

The feminist critic, on the other hand, cannot apply these ideas to the text without first challenging the basic masculinist assumptions behind them; in other words, challenging the weight of Western tradition. Few philosophical ideas will support the feminist model of female as self and male, other. The above-mentioned philosophies cannot be applied to a text without adjustment through change or criticism. By necessity, then, even the major works of Simone de Beauvoir and such a writer as Kate Millett are critical and reactive. If the feminist critic chooses to apply ideas that fit the feminist model for truth about woman, s/he must select from such ideas as personal or collective self-definitions of woman. These obviously carry less intellectual and cultural weight and respectability. The feminist critic has few philosophical shelters, pillars, or guideposts. For all of these reasons, feminist criticism is fraught with intellectual and professional risks, offering more opportunity for creativity, yet greater possibility of error.

If a non-sex-linked idea is applied to a text and related to a masculinist or a feminist reading, the critic's problem is different. For example, if a theatricalist reading is related to a masculinist or feminist reading, the possibilities for interpretation of the text are greatly enriched. In the Giraudoux sentence, if woman is both other *and* actor, then there may be some correlation between actor and other. There may be some consistent denial of actor's self. Actor may always be female and always other. There may be some consistent patterning in the rest of the text which will shed light on the text as a whole that the critic can discover by examining the relationship between the theatricalist idea and the sex-linked idea.

This description of the nature of the critical process and the comparison of masculinist and feminist criticisms would indicate that feminist criticism is not a new type of criticism, but simply a new form of sex-linked criticism, a type of criticism that has been around for a long time as masculinist criticism. By a simple reversal of the dichotomous assumptions that mark sex-linked criticism, feminist criticism has applied a new idea to literature: for the feminist critic, woman is self and man other. The critical process used in this kind of feminist criticism is *not* new, and it is as conservative and as accurate as any other critical method. But while the method is the same, the same means of intellectual support are not always available to the feminist critic; this is probably what makes feminist criticism seem more unorthodox than it actually is.

So far I have suggested some of the basic similarities and differences between some forms of criticism and sex-linked criticism, and between feminist and masculinist criticisms in order to defend feminist criticism as a conservative critical method. What remains to be discussed is the very real radicalism of feminist criticism: what changes it has wrought, what changes are still to come, and what some possibilities are for the future of sex-linked criticism.

If feminist criticism were considered only in the light of the conservative methodology described above and its relatively minor differences from other forms of criticism, it would be difficult to understand the strength of the opposition to it. One must assume that feminist criticism represents some sort of threat to established critical thought if it has such difficulty gaining equal intellectual status with other critical styles.

What feminist critics have accomplished that is new, and perhaps very radical to some, is to reveal by their simple reversal of sex-linked values the very existence of sex-linked criticism and a "school" of masculinist criticism. This is the criticism which has applied those assumptions about woman-as-other that have colored much of literary and critical expression, and until now been unconsciously or un-*self*-consciously held and applied. This discovery is an advance in knowledge about the critical act as it is and has been practiced.

Literary critics, unless they are advocates of a special school of criticism, are not accustomed to examining and revealing their assumptions and methods, but tend simply to present the results of their criticism. Feminist critics' self-conscious awareness, their open struggle with the problems of outlining their own critical method, their new understanding of the sex-linked ideas that critics apply to texts are, while not new to criticism, a challenge to many other critics to examine their own sex-linked ideas. Honest criticism that involves an examination and presentation of the critic's own biases is to be welcomed, and if the practice of feminist criticism has served as a catalyst in this respect it has indeed made a great contribution to the discipline.

Although feminist criticism might seem to threaten what is received by some critics as "truth," it actually cannot threaten the academic critical establishment nor the history of criticism nor critical "truth," if criticism is perceived as a *process of constructing meaning* rather than as a body of knowledge. This would mean that the measure of good criticism is the correctness and completeness of that *process* and not just the correctness of a fixed body of critical "facts."

One of the most interesting and perhaps ultimately the most significant contributions that feminist criticism may make is the understanding that the idea of sex may be seen as simply that—an *idea* in the mind of the writer, and not necessarily something that must be accepted as real. Divisions along the lines of masculine and feminine are abstractions applied to life by those who live it, and applied to literature by those who criticize it. As the idea of God can now be seen as a hypothesis, as values are seen as hypotheses, so male and female can be seen as hypotheses, remnants of a primitive anthropomorphism and simplistic generalities no longer adequate to explain complex new information. The growing realization that Renaissance "humanism" needs to be questioned, that man alone is not the center of the universe, but that woman is there with him, may signal a change in human thought of great significance. When the critic can see maleness and femaleness as hypotheses, s/he is in possession of a powerful new critical perspective and in a position to examine a writer's concept of sex, of male and female, and of the masculine and the feminine as a purely literary system. Feminist criticism is a step on the way to this vision.

NOTES

1. Jean Giraudoux, *Pour Lucrèce* (Paris: Bernard Grasset, 1953), p. 127. The translation is by Schumacher.

2. For an example of the application of an androgynous critical model to literature and a discussion of the distinction between the "androgynous" novel and the "feminist" novel, see Carolyn Heilbrun, *Toward a Recognition of Androgyny* (New York: Alfred A. Knopf, 1973).

CONSCIOUSNESS AND AUTHENTICITY:
TOWARD A FEMINIST AESTHETIC

Marcia Holly

When the idea for a collection of criticism first came to me, I envisioned a book called *Patterns of Strength*, to be comprised of essays analyzing some of the many female literary characters who are self-reliant, independent, strong, courageous—that is, healthy, sane, and mature. I felt that feminists had dwelled long enough on the evils of our low status, lack of prestige, exploitation, and self-abasement. It was time, I thought, to begin rectifying psychological oppression by seeking out and publicizing positive role-models, time to uncover those strong female writers and characters who have been overlooked by literary criticism. How easy it would be, I thought, to counter the stereotyped popular-culture image of women with the realistic and balanced portrayals in significant literature. Hadn't we been taught, after all, that literature is humanist, that it shows the authenticity of lives, of personal psychology, of social interaction? We just needed someone to collect all those studies of real women.

So I sent letters to the 150 or so women whom I knew taught Women and Literature courses, put notices in various women's studies and feminist newsletters, and awaited the deluge of essays showing female patterns of strength. It never came. And gradually I began to see that anticipated deluge for what it was—a desert-mirage. Now, as I reassessed my original plan, I found myself wondering about all those professors who had pronounced literature psychologically real, presenting themselves as humanists unmoved by conventional wisdom and

This essay was adapted for this book from "Introduction: Feminism and Criticism," *Patterns of Strength*, a forthcoming collection of essays edited by Holly.

ideology. I wondered what it would *take* to make literature realistic, literary critics humanist; what it would really *mean* for writers to present us with the "truth" we seek in literature.

Most of the essays that were submitted for my collection tended to deal with the *un*truths about women presented in literature, and with the significance of those untruths. The general tone seemed to be that literature has colluded in encouraging us to isolate ourselves from other women. After all, aren't those *other* women just what the books say they are? Silly, flighty, shrill, illogical, concerned only with childrearing and recipes, inactive—in sum, domestic. We, those supposedly few of us who read, think, reason, learn, converse seriously, and live active and/or creative lives, are so exceptional that we could not possibly relate to other women even if we wanted to, which of course we do not because we have other things on our minds besides ribbons for our bonnets and toilet training—the only topics "those" women are apparently capable of. In other words, those "few" of us who are intelligent females must be neurotic, unfeminine, deviant: the norm, of course, is that which is presented in literature.

The question being formulated here was a revolutionary one: are the truths presented in literature, in fact, *true?* And that question led me to consider what a humanist aesthetic would entail. The single requirement, I reasoned, would be realism, but a realism that might take any form—fantasy, epic, narrative, lyric—since *non*realism in regard to women has taken every form. This realism would not complacently accept the standard sexual myths and stereotypes, but would be excavational, would do for women what, I am tempted to say, such writers as Tolstoy, Joyce, Sartre, and Camus have done for men. But I am not at all certain that men have been treated realistically either. Although men have been given a feeling of self-worth and legitimacy, that feeling is all too often based on stereotypes of masculinity and is surely based on a class structure. Nevertheless, first-rank male authors do reinforce self-questioning and personal struggle in men; they accept the fact that men are seeking fulfillment and growth, and that men confront difficult personal and social conflicts. There is a lack of an equivalent reinforcement for women. Part of realism is to represent the soul-searching that literature now reserves as another privilege of the already privileged white middle- and upper-class male.

It is not sufficient to say that literature must be realistic without first explaining what I mean by the term. But before I attempt that definition, I would like to share a classroom anecdote. Near the end of a course on American literature, in which I had often dealt with literary manifestations of racism and sexism, one of my students pointed out that I had been far more critical of female than of male, of black than of white writers. Why had I treated F. Scott Fitzgerald's racism sympathetically and put it into context, but questioned Phyllis Wheatley's patriotic poems? It was a perceptive observation that caused me to search my aesthetics as well as my soul. Was it a manifestation of my own sexism-racism? I think not. When Fitzgerald expresses a racist psychology through his dramatizations and imagery, it might indicate a lack of creative vision but it need not indicate bad faith. He is not being dishonest in his presentation so much as limited in his world view. He may have searched his soul and dramatized what he found. Thus he can be criticized sociologically but not necessarily artistically.

Wheatley, on the other hand, praises a society for its freedom when she, a slave, could not possibly have known freedom (in spite of having been privileged enough to learn to read). To be truthful she would have had to deal with some of the pain of not being free in a society verbally committed to human dignity and freedom.

Is it necessary, then, to know a writer's background in order to criticize her/his work? Yes and no. To determine whether or not a person has written in bad faith, we must indeed know about her/his life. But to determine its psychological authenticity we need only have the work and an unbiased understanding of human needs, motivations, and emotions. Both positions require movement away from formalist criticism and insist that we judge by standards of authenticity. This latter approach, furthermore, requires that we as readers (and critics) question our own biases and assumptions. If we believe that women are adjuncts to men and incapable of acting independently, then we will probably find such a character as Emma Woodhouse unrealistic or unlikeable, while Emma Bovary will come across as an archetype.

Accurate criticism, then, must follow what is called "consciousness-raising." That is, in order to recognize sexual stereotyping and authenticity in a literary work, we must first bring to a conscious level our own fundamental and perhaps erroneous beliefs about the nature, character, and destiny of women. Critics become humanist only when they formulate their critiques after reaching an honest appraisal of their own ideologies, and supplement this by the development of insights about human reality gained from a variety of disciplines. Literary criticism, like social science, can begin to be objective only when critics are informed about prevailing cultural myths, about the sexual, racial, and religious stereotypes that we as a people have internalized, and are therefore at the core of our hypotheses.

The critic in her/his capacity as analyst and interpreter is responsible for admitting and understanding any biases s/he maintains. Critics not only make value judgments but often establish the limits of meaning for a work; that is, the critic and/or teacher can set the terms within which a work is questioned, thereby establishing the boundaries of potential response. It then takes a rare reader to pose questions outside those limits. Ideally, of course, a critic raises all possible questions about the meaning and value of a work, but in reality the critic is limited by her/his personal and experiential vision. A Norman Mailer, for example, who posits the masculinist ethos that a woman's highest purpose is as a receptacle for the omnipotent sperm, cannot be expected to question the reality of such a character as Hemingway's Brett Ashley. Nor can he be expected to evaluate the impact of *The Sun Also Rises* on women.

A less obvious example of critical consensus limiting potential response concerns Joyce's *Ulysses*. Few critics have questioned the authenticity or effect of Molly Bloom; in fact, the standard analysis treats her as a paradigm of sensuality. A feminist critic, however, might find Molly sensually inadequate because her sensuality exists not for herself but for the men to whom she reacts. She does not have a moral, intellectual, emotional, or sexual life of her own; hence, she is not authentically sensual but, to use Cynthia Griffin Wolff's term, "a mirror for men."[1] Because Molly represents only a male fantasy of sensuality and not what a truly sensual woman is or might be, it is an error to define her as a realistic portrayal. And by defining her as real, typical, or archetypal, critics impose on us a narrow range of responses. The reader who says "no" to Molly's "yes" thinks of herself, again, as deviant or intellectually limited for being unable to see the depths of Molly's character. In order to have an acceptable view of Molly Bloom, the reader is forced into dishonesty or encouraged to deny the authenticity of herself and her life.

Similar in effect and equally significant is the critical exclusion of women from humanity. One example of such critical monocularity is Terence Martin's recent analysis of Ken Kesey's *One Flew over the Cuckoo's Nest*.[2] Martin appropriately interprets the novel as the study of a struggle to reach masculinity. Martin does not, however, differentiate between maleness and manhood which leads him into a monochromatic view. Martin shows that throughout the novel the real enemy is woman, who is depicted as emasculating, bitchy, the destroyer of life and energy. Yet he finds the novel "sanative and cleansing" (p. 44). He finds that the novel "is an intense statement about the high cost of living" which, and the emphasis is mine, "will remain true for [Chief Bromden] *and for all of us*" (p. 55). Well, Mr. Martin, it isn't true for *women*. What Martin does in his essay is to assume that all humanity, all readers, are male. That assumption is obviously biased, limited, and incorrect. Yet a likely-to-be-accepted interpretation is based entirely on that misperception of reality.

Martin's analysis is posited on his acceptance of Kesey's allegory as a literal hypothesis: that *human* life problems stem from emasculating female authority. By not questioning this hypothesis, by not suggesting that it is an inaccurate and inapplicable perception, Martin fails to evaluate the novel within a human context and thus perpetuates the ideology that all people are male.

Feminist critics, by recognizing ourselves as women, are in the process of balancing that kind of lopsided view of humanity and reality. We are questioning and analyzing the depictions of women and the treatments of women's lives in literature. We are searching for a truly revolutionary art. The content of a given piece need not be feminist, of course, for that piece to be humanist, and therefore revolutionary. Revolutionary art is that which roots out the essentials about the human condition rather than perpetuating false ideologies.[3]

Surely no feminist or humanist critic could see *One Flew over the Cuckoo's Nest* as a realistic symbol of the human condition. My concern here is not to dispute Kesey's thesis, but to criticize the book in terms of what might be considered *realistic*. Realism first of all demands a consistent (noncontradictory) perception of those issues (emotions, motivations, conflicts) to which the work has been limited. *One Flew over the Cuckoo's Nest* is concerned with emasculation, the destruction of male energy and vitality; and Kesey *begins* to perceive a legitimate cause when he characterizes the destructive element as "the Combine," offering by way of illustration the demoralization of Indians by government forces, and the degradation of workers by the factory. But instead of defining and struggling with the make-up of *the Combine*, Kesey abrogates his responsibility to the question at hand and symbolizes the Combine as a *woman*—this, although neither of the institutions he has mentioned have anything to do with female domination. Such facile personification not only represents the struggle in terms of a false analogy, forcing Kesey to posit assumptions not germane to the issues he has raised, but by doing so, serves to perpetuate the myth behind the analogy: the Pandora fantasy—all women create evil, all women wish to destroy men, all of life's ills are caused by matriarchy. Witness Martin, who not only accepted it as a working hypothesis, but based his analysis upon it![4]

When a work is concerned primarily with male-female relationships or the delineation of the female character, realism demands that the perceptions dramatized go beyond inapplicable clichés to suggest authentic rather than apparent motivations. Virginia Woolf, for example, in creating Lily Briscoe in *To the Lighthouse* indicates that Mrs. Ramsay's sensitivity and Mr. Ramsay's abstract intellectuality are not givens of the sexes. Lily unifies in herself those qualities typically assigned as sex traits. In fact, the burden of the book seems to be that personal wholeness develops with and from the dialectical integration of qualities seen as opposing. Because Woolf sets herself the task of illuminating male-female character and interaction, the measurement for her success is whether she accepts cultural definitions or seeks to go beyond them into what is human. Conversely, Hemingway's work must be distrusted from the outset, not simply because he debases women and glorifies masculinity, but because within his self-imposed limitation of defining masculinity and femininity he fails to transcend superficial cultural definitions. Since they are the area he confines himself to dramatizing, he must be judged on the perceptivity of those definitions.

The sexism of Milton, no less severe than that of Hemingway or Kesey, does not require the rejection of his poetry for the reason that he does not focus exclusively on male-female interaction or character. Nor is he guilty of Kesey's simplistic attribution of all human ills to women. On one level Milton does, of course, blame Eve for the acceptance of evil. However, he manages to go beyond that view to show the effects of chaos on all people. Those aspects of *Paradise Lost* that are demeaning to women are not the only, or even the primary, aspects of his work or his contribution. Milton's task was to consider both the chaos-evil and paradise within, a human theme as applicable to women as to men. Although critics should point out that Milton did not judge the two sexes by the same criteria, whether or not he saw the conflict in the same terms for Eve as for Adam matters less than that the conflict exists for all human beings. Thus women too can identify with the theme; however, because Milton's bias is not usually asserted in the classroom, women too often find themselves rejecting the valid (that is, essentially human) themes as well as the invalid (sexist-moralizing) aspects of *Paradise Lost*. With Hemingway, identification with the theme is impossible since he treats exclusively male conflicts: his books are concerned with men achieving socially defined traits which by definition exclude women. Stated in the extreme, Hemingway's themes, like Kesey's, revolve around how to be *masculine* (*macho*), not how to be human.

In realistic literature, the writer presents androgynous themes that are worked out with creative insight, apart from considerations of gender. That does not mean, of course, that realism excludes sex and sexuality, but that it treats sex and sex-related issues from a human rather than a masculine perspective. E. M. Forster's *Maurice* (New York: Norton, 1971) for example, dramatizes sexuality in terms of legitimate human conflict and focuses on discrepant power in ways that women as well as men can respond to. Treating male sexual concerns and feelings from a male point of view is also legitimate, but the fact needs to be made clear that the view is male and not global.

In general, the sex of characters ought not to control the humanness of their conflicts. The character of Ophelia, for instance, and her relationship to Hamlet does not undermine the essential human theme of the play, a tragedy that must be judged on how authentically the problem of inertia is dramatized. That Hamlet's conflict need not be gender-specific is one aspect of the tragedy's greatness.[5]

When we are dealing, then, with literature in which sexuality is dramatized within the context of an androgynous theme, the standard for judgment is how well a writer presents the *human* condition, a judgment that a critic can make only after s/he differentiates between what is derived from an arbitrary ideology and what is an authentic concern of people.

However, when a writer does focus on male-female interaction or on female or male psychology, the writer is to be judged by her/his assumptions about women and men. We reject facile answers in works that treat non-sex-related topics: we find Horatio Alger ludicrous because he presents an invalid personal solution to social questions; we accept Dickens because he presents human social conditions as social conditions; we cannot accept the validity or truth of literature that exhibits no understanding of male-female power relationships when concerned with male-female interaction.

Our criticism, then, must take into account what areas of life the writer has selected as her/his terrain. Within that terrain, perceptions must be exhibited that are not controlled by ideology, and it is this standard by which we must judge both creators and critics. The critic must be held responsible for questioning her/his adherence to sex, class, and race biases in evaluating a work; the writer must be held accountable for creating superficial and stereotyped characters or motivations. Understanding the pervasive sexist ideology and its manifestations in literature is of particular significance because the great percentage of our literature does concern itself with human interaction. Thus, although some literature is exempt, most must be considered within the context of what is true about sex-traits and what are unthinking, myopic, and male-serving assumptions.

This aesthetic position is not a closed "party line." Feminist critical essays vary, although there are some universal positions that feminists hold. Each feminist critic, for example, has undergone consciousness-raising, which enables her to see herself as a woman in a male-oriented society. And each critic expresses an understanding that literature has failed generally to create authentic female characters.

The activity of literary criticism is no longer so simple as it was. Like most thoughtful communication, it has become a political act. We now recognize that literature, and the media in general, significantly influence our daily lives by creating role-models and patterns of interaction. Therefore, the media—directly, and indirectly through critical evaluation—effect power relationships. Literature has a most immediate impact on us, and the critics represented in *Patterns of Strength* are concerned that that impact not continue to collude in society's oppression of women.

Patterns of Strength, therefore, is an appropriate title: it refers to the critics rather than to what they have discovered in the literature. We have begun to identify ourselves as women, and to reject the prevailing literary judgments because those judgments do not reflect our reality. Feminist criticism is our attempt to find a congenial critical method, one that unites subjective responses, self-knowledge, and objective "scientific" analysis. It is a courageous attempt, unconventional, and ultimately revolutionary. For this reason, our work has become integrally bound with our lives; and because we are involved in changing our lives, in discovering alternatives for women, our criticism is not abstract—it is immediate, concrete, emergent, even unpolished.

Susanne Langer points out, in *Philosophy in a New Key*, that what characterizes a school, a movement, or an age is the formulation of problems, and that to reject a question is to repudiate the very framework of the questioner's thinking, the orientation of her/his mind, the assumptions s/he has always entertained as common-sense notions about things in general.[6] Feminist criticism represents the repudiation of previous formulations about women. It has emerged from a radical perspective about literature and sex roles, and is a tentative beginning in the development of a feminist literary aesthetic—one that is fundamentally at odds with masculinist value standards, measuring literature against an understanding of authentic female life. Feminist criticism is therefore a stage in the development of literary criticism and indicates that we, as women, have begun to take ourselves and our culture quite seriously.

NOTES

1. Cynthia Griffin Wolff, "A Mirror for Men: Stereotypes of Women in Literature," *Woman: An Issue*, ed. Lee R. Edward, Mary Heath, and Lisa Baskin (Boston: Little, Brown, 1972), pp. 205-18.

2. Terence Martin, "*One Flew over the Cuckoo's Nest* and the High Cost of Living," *Modern Fiction Studies* 19(Spring 1973):43-55.

3. An excellent presentation of this point is made by Georg Lukàcs in his essay "Marx and Engels on Aesthetics," *Writer and Critic* (New York: Grosset and Dunlap, 1971):

Humanism, that is, the passionate study of man's nature, is essential to all literature and art; and good art and good literature are humanistic to the extent that they not only investigate man and the real essence of his nature with passion but also and simultaneously defend human integrity passionately against all attacks, degradation and distortion. Since such tendencies (especially the oppression and exploitation of man by man) attain such a level of inhumanity in no other society as under capitalism just because of the objective reification we have mentioned, every true artist, every true writer as a creative individual is instinctively an enemy of this distortion of the principle of humanism, whether consciously or not [p. 69].

Lukàcs differentiates between naturalistic art and "real art" which "represents life in its totality, in motion, development and evolution" (p. 77), and places art within the context of the historical process. It is worth reading his essay to understand how he places art within the dialectic of appearance and reality, defining thereby the revolutionary qualities inherent in "real art."

4. The matriarchy is nonexistent both in actuality and in the novel. Big Nurse is merely *allowed* to run the ward by the incompetent doctor who is her superior. An accurate appraisal of the forces emasculating men and an analysis of the myth of matriarchy is presented by Eve Merriam in the section of her book *After Nora Slammed the Door* reprinted as "The Matriarchal Myth" in *Up against the Wall, Mother . . .* , ed. Elsie Adams and Mary Louise Briscoe (Beverly Hills, California: Glencoe, 1971), pp. 213-22. Merriam shows that the fairy tale of Big Momma having all the power in our society serves to conceal the actuality: that the Corporations determine our destinies and that their success can be linked to their imposing the matriarchal myth even as they place men in that relationship to the Company usually assigned to wives. That Kesey and Martin do not see the full implications of the Combine is an unfortunate indication that they, too, have fallen prey to the capitalist mythology.

5. It might be argued that *Hamlet* is too class-specific to be universal because Hamlet's problems relate to power that is restricted to ruling class (white) males. However, the serious themes of *Hamlet* are not exclusively ruling class nor male nor white, but human.

6. Susanne Langer, *Philosophy in a New Key*, 3d ed. (Cambridge: Harvard University Press, 1971), pp. 3-7.

VIRGINIA WOOLF'S CRITICISM:
A POLEMICAL PREFACE

Barbara Currier Bell & Carol Ohmann

In her novels, and those are what most of her readers know best, Virginia Woolf habitually aims at creating moments of freedom, moments when the self, breaking bonds and vaulting bounds, arrives at an unqualified intensity of thought and emotion. Clarissa Dalloway, on a London morning in spring, feels herself lifted on "waves of divine vitality." "It [is] very, very dangerous," she thinks, but without any regret, "to live even one day." Lily Briscoe, toward the close of *To the Lighthouse*, is oppressed by Mr. Ramsay's demands: he is a widower, and hence aggrieved; she is a woman and owes him, he would insist, solace. She cannot, she will not oblige: she'd gotten up that morning to paint. But suddenly, forgetting him and forgetting herself, she sees, and remarks, that his boots are beautiful. For the moment Lily and Mr. Ramsay are unlocked from the past and convention. They reach, together, "the blessed island of good boots." Percival, in *The Waves*, has a power over the other characters that may surely be tied to the image he appears to present of perfectly habitual, perfectly unconscious self-expression. He need not study Shakespeare's plays; he simply understands them; he appears to be at home, and at large, in a brave new world. And even Eleanor Pargiter, in *The Years*, wakes from the constriction of nearly a lifetime to ask, "And now? . . . And now?" She is at once ripe and ready.

As a novelist, Virginia Woolf has taken, and takes, some wrist-slapping. By some of her contemporaries she was viewed, as E. M.

Reprinted from *Critical Inquiry*, vol. 1, no. 1 (Chicago: University of Chicago Press, 1974).

Forster said, in an image that condensed many a small-minded complaint: she was viewed as the Invalid Lady of Bloomsbury. And we have heard that just a few seasons ago, when the idea was first put to them, the committee of assorted academic eminences that plans the programs for the English Institute said no to a suggestion for a series of papers on Woolf; she was, some of them asserted, not good enough for the Institute, which has traditionally assembled at Columbia and, most recently, at Harvard. But time may do much and indeed has already done very much to praise Virginia Woolf as the creator of *Mrs. Dalloway, To the Lighthouse, The Waves,* and *Between the Acts.*

Our purpose is to discuss her criticism, and at the same time to praise, even to celebrate, that.* Her criticism is less well known than her fiction. It's been neglected, and deserves much more attention than it's gotten.[1] In passing, we might make the guess—we consider it quite a reasonable one—that it has been easier for professional academics to praise, or even only to notice, a woman novelist, than it has been to accept a woman critic.

As a critic, Virginia Woolf has been called a number of disparaging names: "impressionist," "bellelettrist," "raconteur," "amateur." Here is one academic talking on the subject: "She will survive, not as a critic, but as a literary essayist recording the adventures of a soul among congenial masterpieces. . . . The writers who are most downright, and masculine, and central in their approach to life—a Fielding or a Balzac—she for the most part left untouched. . . . Her own approach was at once more subterranean and aerial, and invincibly, almost defiantly, feminine."[2] In other words: Virginia Woolf is not a critic; how could she be? She is a woman. From its beginning, criticism has been a man's world. This is to say not only that males have earned their living as critics, but, more importantly, that the conventionally accepted ideals of critical method are linked with qualities stereotypically allotted to males: analysis, judgment, objectivity. Virginia Woolf has had a poor reputation as a critic not merely because her sex was female, but because her method is "feminine." She writes in a way that is said to be creative, appreciative, and subjective. We will accept this description for

*We should like at the start to thank our Wesleyan colleagues Victor Vogt and Phyllis Rose; they read this article in manuscript and offered us a number of helpful suggestions.

the moment, but will later enlarge on it, and even our provisional acceptance we mean to turn to a compliment.

Virginia Woolf's difference from conventional critics is precisely one reason, we would argue, why she should be praised. She is not almost defiantly feminine; she is beyond a doubt defiantly feminine. She is in revolt against the established terms and tones of literary study. Researching for a book on literary history, she had this experience, which she records in her diary:

> Yesterday in the Public Library I took down a book of X.'s criticism. This turned me against writing my book. London Library atmosphere effused. Turned me against all literary criticism: these so clever, so airless, so fleshless ingenuities and attempts to prove—that T. S. Eliot for example is a worse critic than X. Is all literary criticism that kind of exhausted air?—book dust, London Library, air. Or is it only that X, is a second hand, frozen fingered, university specialist, don trying to be creative, don all stuffed with books, writer? . . . I dipped for five minutes and put the book back depressed. The man asked, "What do you want, Mrs. Woolf?" I said a history of English literature. But was so sickened I couldn't look. There were so many.[3]

Or again, she writes:

> [Do not] let us shy away from the kings because we are commoners. That is a fatal crime in the eyes of Aeschylus, Shakespeare, Virgil, and Dante, who, if they could speak—and after all they can—would say, "Don't leave me to the wigged and gowned. Read me, read me for yourselves." They do not mind if we get our accents wrong, or have to read with a crib in front of us. Of course—are we not commoners, outsiders?—we shall trample many flowers and bruise much ancient grass. . . . [But] let us trespass at once. Literature is no one's private ground; literature is common ground.[4]

No other twentieth century critic has approached literature with less explicit "system" and more sympathy than Virginia Woolf. Trespassers, she knew, had to stay aloof from all critical schools, to differ from them all. In her diary, she frequently expressed a wish to break new ground.

I feel . . . at the back of my brain that I can devise a new critical method; something far less still and formal than [what has been done before] . . . . There must be some simpler, subtler, closer means of writing about books, as about people, could I hit upon it.[5]

Although she was never finally satisfied with herself, she did write criticism that is truly revolutionary. In what follows, we will try to describe the most significant terms of her revolt.

She solves, first of all, the problem of how to address her readers amiably and unpretentiously, and her solution is crucial to her overall success as a critic. For she is not traditionally authoritarian, not an eminence, not a lecturer in her mode of relationship to her audience. Instead of the stance of omniscience, which is a stance that is often uncongenial to women writers (it never did Charlotte Brontë any good, Emily avoided it, and George Eliot assumed it with success only, perhaps, because her dominant emotional tone was one of suffering compassion and hence not altogether at odds with conventional requirements for women)—instead of the stance of omniscience, Woolf invents "the common reader," and employs that *persona* convincingly. When she says "we," she means *we*, rhetorically asserting the existence of a community, but, in fact, by that rhetoric and the other devices we will note, working to create a community.

"We" are readers, not critics or scholars. "We" are English men and women who read for pleasure and for inspiration when "we" can get it. "We" are tolerant but not permissive; "we" laugh and cry but "we" are not fickle, "our" sentiments have limits; "we" believe in common virtues; "we" like fantasy in measurable doses; "we" are worldly-wise but not world-weary; "we" are of "our" age but ours could be any age;[6] "we" constantly question and argue with writers the minute they assume too much, or pretend wisdom, or get too far from the facts of daily life. "['We' are] guided by an instinct to create for ['ourselves'], out of whatever odds and ends ['we'] can come by, some kind of whole—a portrait of a man, a sketch of an age, a theory of the art of writing."[7] But "we" do not like labels. "We" do not care about the difference between the pre-Romantics and the post-Romantics, or between a novelist of manners and a novelist of sentiment. "We" may, in the end, accept assumptions, or morals, or fantasies, but not without good reason. "We" are suspicious of books "for we have our own vision of the world; we have made it from our own experience and prejudices, and it is therefore bound up with our own vanities and loves. It is impossible not to feel injured and insulted if tricks are played and our private harmony is upset."[8] When we do make a judgment, we make it forthrightly and simply.

> The Edwardians have developed a technique of novel-writing which suits their purpose; they have made tools and established conventions which do their business. But those tools are not our tools, and that business is not our business. For us those conventions are ruin, those tools are death.[9]

Her "common reader" helps Woolf to produce critical essays that are exceptionally readable, clear, and vivid. Thanks to "us," her essays move smoothly and quickly, for the common reader's reactions seem to dictate most of her commentary, even though the truth, of course, is exactly the opposite: she has shaped or elicited the reactions she posits.[10] Her continual consciousness of "the common reader" is especially useful to Woolf in essays on abstract aesthetic topics. "We" prevent her from becoming too general, or pedantic, or confusing. "We" ask hard questions like "What is art?" or "How should one read a book?" and demand outright answers. Also, "we" are a source that generates imagery. Woolf, of course, uses a great deal of imagery in her criticism; the fact has been often observed, but by no means (or seldom) connected with the common reader. First of all, we like imagery. In an effort to please us, Woolf uses it as liberally as cooks use seasoning. Second, we need imagery. Many of the ideas Woolf puts forth, particularly in the aesthetic essays, are essentially abstruse, and images are the fastest, most concrete and effective means of explanation—that is, if they are of a certain kind: either simple, or striking, or both.[11]

An essay titled "The Elizabethan Lumber Room" will do as an extended example here.[12] It offers an introduction to Woolf's favorite period, discussing the *zeitgeist*, the quires of poetry, prose, and drama, and their characteristic evolution. It might be a syllabus for a seminar at Columbia or Harvard. But it is more winning than most seminars. It offers a highly imaginative alternative to conventional literary criticism.

The essay is a review of Hakluyt's famous book, *Early Voyages, Travels, and Discoveries of the English Nation*. In her very first sentence, Woolf puts herself on our level of acknowledging, "These magnificent volumes are not often, perhaps, read through." We nod. We have not often, or even ever read through Hakluyt; we do belong in the community that Woolf invokes. Then, Woolf involves us further with her metaphor of the lumber room; it is exactly the simple and striking kind of image we like and need:

> [Hakluyt] is not so much a book as a great bundle of commodities loosely tied together, an emporium, a lumber room strewn with ancient sacks, obsolete nautical instruments, huge bales of wool, and little bags of rubies and emeralds. One is for ever untying this packet here, sampling that heap over there, wiping the dust off some vast map of the world, and sitting down in semi-darkness to snuff the strange smells of silks and leathers and ambergris, while outside tumble the huge waves of the uncharted Elizabethan sea.

Hakluyt's expeditions, Woolf goes on to tell us, were manned by "apt young men" who loved to explore and trade for treasure. They told the mysterious and wondrous tales that Hakluyt recorded as truth. Here, knowing our liking not only for imagery but also for narrative, Woolf tells us some of these tales.

> The Earl of Cumberland's men, hung up by adverse winds off the coast of Cornwall for a fortnight, licked the muddy water off the deck in agony. And sometimes a ragged and wornout man came knocking at the door of an English country house and claimed to be the boy who had left it years ago to sail the seas. . . . He had with him a black stone, veined with gold, or an ivory tusk, or a silver ingot, and urged on the village youth with talk of gold strewn over the land as stones are strewn in the fields of England.

At one level, Woolf is entertaining us, but at another, she is instructing us, for these tales were, after all, a major source for Elizabethan literature. "All this," she writes, "the new words, the new ideas, the waves, the savages, the adventures, found their way naturally into the plays which were being acted on the banks of the Thames." The extravagant spirit that fabricated them is the same extravagant spirit

that buoys us up through so many Elizabethan writings. In the words of
the essay:

> Thus, with singing and with music, springs into existence the
> characteristic Elizabethan extravagance; the dolphins and lavoltas
> of Greene; the hyperbole, more surprising in a writer so terse and
> muscular, of Ben Jonson. Thus we find the whole of Elizabethan
> literature strewn with gold and silver; with talk of Guiana's
> rarities, and references to that America . . . which was not merely
> a land on the map but symbolized the unknown territories of the
> soul.

The next section of the essay, in which Woolf weighs two important
Elizabethan genres against each other, effortlessly continues from her
opening metaphor. The magic spirit of the lumber room inspired
poetry, but was bad for prose. She writes, "Rhyme and metre helped
the poets to keep the tumult of their perceptions in order. But the
prose writer, without these restrictions, accumulated clauses, petered
out interminable catalogues, tripped and stumbled over the convolu-
tions of his own rich draperies." From this point, Woolf moves to the
next with another image, "The stage was the nursery where prose learnt
to find its feet."

Now, having covered prose, poetry, and drama, and having explained
the reason for drama's importance, she begins slowly to trace the
evolution *out* of Elizabethan literature: "The publicity of the stage and
the perpetual presence of a second person, were hostile to that growing
consciousness of one's self . . . which, as the years went by, sought
expression." As necessarily as a pendulum swing, the pressure of the
outside world caused writers to reflect upon themselves, but with the
old imagery intact. Woolf quotes Sir Thomas Browne: " 'The world
that I regard is myself; it is the microcosm of my own frame that I cast
mine eye on; for the other I use it but like my globe, and turn it round
sometimes for my recreation.' " " 'We carry with us the wonders we
seek without us; there is all Africa and her prodigies in us.' " She leads
us to sympathize with Browne: she involves us with her picture of him
in the same way she involved us with her picture of Hakluyt, his covers
shut before his conclusion. "In short, as we say when we cannot help
laughing at the oddities of people we admire most, he was a character,
and the first to make us feel that the most sublime speculations of the

human imagination are issued from a particular man, whom we can love." Again, we nod; we identify; we fully consent to her use of "we." At the very end of her essay, Woolf repeats the lumber room metaphor. Only now, instead of being an image for Hakluyt's book—the outside world that so excited Elizabethans—it is an image for the mind of Sir Thomas Browne—the inside world that so intrigued writers of the seventeenth century. "Now," she writes, "we are in the presence of sublime imagination; now rambling through one of the finest lumber rooms in the world—a chamber stuffed from floor to ceiling with ivory, old iron, broken pots, urns, unicorns' horns, and magic glasses full of emerald lights and blue mystery." The lumber room has served to beguile us in the beginning of the essay, to guide us throughout, and to give us a rich sense of unity at the end. Yet, like the symbols of great poetry, it has never preached to us directly.

Though "the common reader" was Virginia Woolf's most dramatic critical innovation—and probably the most important to *her*—she made other experiments in criticism to escape tradition. She pushed, for example, a certain kind of biographical criticism to its frontier. "Try to become the author," she advises herself, and thinks further, "Were I another person I would say to myself, Please write criticism; biography; invent a new form for both."[13] Woolf's search for a new combination of criticism and biography might be thought of as representing her attachment to that old critical dictum, "The style is the man." In a number of her essays, she personifies the works of a writer; so she presents us not with a series of texts but with some*one*, a man or a woman.

She makes a person, for instance, out of Goldsmith's essays, and calls the person Goldsmith. "The Citizen [in Goldsmith's volume *The Citizen of the World*] is still a most vivacious companion as he takes his walk from Charing Cross to Ludgate Hill . . . Goldsmith keeps just on the edge of the crowd so we can hear what the common people are saying and note their humours. Shrewdly and sarcastically he casts his eye, as he saunters on, upon the odd habits and sights that the English are so used to that they no longer see them."[14] The point is that "Goldsmith," in this passage, is actually Goldsmith's book.

Woolf had sense enough to think about the appropriateness of her technique carefully, so that the debate about biographical criticism has been enriched by her thoughts. Considering Henley, a man who, accord-

ing to her, wrote the most mechanical sort of biographical criticism, she
said, "There are times when we would sweep aside all biography and all
psychology for the sake of a single song or a single poem expounded
and analysed phrase-by-phrase."[15] Finally in favor of her biographical
tendencies as a critic, however, she said that a writer never stops being a
writer, even when he does not write; "the pith and essence of [a
person's] character . . . shows itself to the observant eye in the tone of
a voice, the turn of a head, some little phrase or anecdote picked up in
passing."[16] If the tiniest, vaguest clues can show a person's essence,
then Woolf was surely justified in reading from book to author and
back again. In her essay "Personalities," she analyzes again her brand of
criticism, offering the following justification and quite sensible reserva-
tion about it:

> The people whom we admire most as writers . . . have something
> elusive, enigmatic, impersonal about them. . . . In ransacking their
> drawers we shall find out little about them. All has been distilled
> into their books. The life is thin, modest, colourless, like blue
> skimmed milk at the bottom of the jar. It is the imperfect artists
> who never manage to say the whole thing in their books who
> wield the power of personality over us.[17]

In other words, bringing the life of the writer *to* the work or deducing
personality *from* a work may be more or less appropriate, more or less
revelatory, according to the nature of the biography or the *oeuvre*
under scrutiny. Woolf may not have succeeded in inventing a new form
in her mixture of biography and criticism: at the least, we remember
Johnson's *Lives of the Poets*, Lamb's *Essays of Elia*, or Hazlitt's *Table
Talk*, and we may even recall *Hours in a Library*, written by Sir Leslie
Stephen, Woolf's father. She did, however, overtake her predecessors in
the devotion and the grace with which she practised it.

Of course, Woolf habitually moved out of criticism coupled with
biography into pure biography. Many of her essays review letters,
memoirs, autobiographies, biographies. Her interest in these latter
stretches further, and is a further instance of her revolt against tradition: she writes repeatedly on works outside the standard canon of
English literature. She suggests that the word "literature" might well be
redefined, as we find it undergoing redefinition today, to include
popular or miscellaneous writing of all periods.[18] And she takes women

writers quite seriously, going out of the conventional way to notice them and give notice of them. Roughly 20 percent of her published essays are about women writers directly. Roughly the same proportion again are indirectly concerned with the frustrating limits that conventional society places on women's personal and literary lives. An essay on Dorothy Osborne's *Letters*, for example, stresses that the literary talents of women could only begin, historically, to find expression in what we might call "underground" writing. In "Madame de Sévigné," she looks anew at a famous "token woman"; in "Sara Coleridge," sketches the difficulties of a literary daughter; and in "Poe's Helen," emphasizes Helen far more than Poe.

The features of Woolf's criticism we have been concerned with are all, we would argue, strategies in a single campaign: an effort to take books down from library shelves and put them into the hands of her ideal community, the common readers. And to talk about them outside the walls of lecture rooms. And to talk about them, finally, in such a way that they matter, not in literary history, but in our lives.

Woolf has, as we noted at the beginning, been called "subjective," and we accepted the term with its apparently pejorative overtones. But the acceptance was only temporary, and we want now to return to it so as to redefine it.

In 1923, beginning to revise a number of essays for publication in the collection she titled *The Common Reader*, Woolf wrote in her diary, "I shall really investigate literature with a view to answering certain questions about ourselves."[19] Not "myself," but "ourselves." She is not a subjective critic in the sense that she refers to her own life in her critical essays.[20] She does not, for instance, mention that she knew some of the contemporary authors she wrote about; and, as an early biographer remarked, "No one would guess from reading 'The Enchanted Organ' that the woman whose selected letters she was reviewing had been not only Miss Thackeray, Mrs. Richmond Ritchie but also Aunt Annie [the sister of Sir Leslie Stephen's first wife]."[21] It would be impossible to learn from Woolf's criticism about her daily routine or her friends or her marriage or her mental illness or her work for the Women's Cooperative Guild. Yet her work may be called subjective in this broader sense, that she sees literature as a series of personal transactions, a series of encounters between people writing and people reading, and she urges us to see both literature and popular culture that way ourselves.

Learning, she knows, is by no means necessarily a humanizing experience. In the biography of Dr. Bentley, head of Trinity College, Cambridge, she tells us, Bentley is described as extraordinarily learned, knowing Homer by heart, reading Sophocles and Pindar the way we read newspapers and magazines, spending his life largely in the company of the greatest of the Greeks. And yet, in his life, she says, "we shall [also] find much that is odd and little that is reassuring. . . . The man who should have been steeped in beauty (if what they say of the Classics is true) as a honey-pot is ingrained with sweetness was, on the contrary, the most quarrelsome of mankind."[22] He was aggressive; he was coercive; he bullied and threatened his academic staff at Trinity and beyond a doubt did the same to students. Did the Society of Trinity College dare to think he spent too much of the college funds on the staircase of his own lodging? Did they perceive that he stole food, drink and fuel from the college stores? Then let them look at their jobs and their other preferments. And so on and on and on.

Nonetheless, Woolf's essays imply, over and over again, that learning can be a humanizing experience. And here we turn back to our beginning. Far from merely recording the adventures of a soul among masterpieces, Woolf's criticism always exerts a standard of judgment, seldom explicit but nonetheless there, informing her essays, evident in the selection of her details as well as the choices of her *persona* and her rhetoric. In *A Room of One's Own*, she speaks of Shakespeare's mind as a mind without "obstacle," a mind "unimpeded" and "incandescent," free to produce works of art. Such works "seem to stand there complete by themselves," which is to say not only that form and content beautifully accord, but that the works do not break or unseam to show, say, an anger that is only personal or a grievance merely local. And John Paston, reading in Norfolk with the sea to his left and the fen to his right, saw in Chaucer fields and skies and people he recognized, but seldom rendered more brightly, more clearly, "rounded and complete." Chaucer's mind, too, was "free to apply its force fully to its object."[23] On the other hand, reading Charlotte Brontë's novels,[24] Woolf finds material not germane to fictional design, not consistent with the predominant point of view and style. There are interpolations of self-defense and interjections of indignation—indignation about, for example, the lot of the English governess. The explanation for these anomalies, Woolf suggests, can be found by moving back beyond the work of art to the mind that made it, and there is the life "cramped and thwarted," pressed into uncongenial services and attitudes that frustrated the impulse of genius to express itself, "whole and entire." While Woolf's criticism of Brontë is in some ways adverse, it is, nonetheless, basically sympathetic. What was, evokes hauntingly the image of what might have been. And more, what should have been. The critical ideal applied to Shakespeare, Chaucer and Brontë is the same ideal of the free self that Woolf expresses in her novels, a self breaking bonds and vaulting bounds, a self arriving at the furthest intensity of thought and emotion.

In this last sense, then, Woolf's criticism may without injury be called subjective or personal. Its function is to humanize our lives, to urge a liberation and wholeness of self. It is a brilliant and graceful protest against any narrower, more abstract, or merely professional critical purpose. To put the case concretely, as she habitually did, it is a brilliant and graceful protest against one of the pictures she drew in *A Room of One's Own:* Professor von X., engaged in writing a "monumental work." Professor von X. is heavy in build, his eyes are very small, his complexion is red with anger, and he "jabs" with his pen at his paper "as if he were killing some noxious insect."[25]

NOTES

1. Not many readers of Woolf know how *much* criticism she published: somewhere near 400 articles. Her first publications were reviews, and at certain times in her life she financed her novels with her criticism. Of her critical work, produced for leading journals and sometimes anonymous, only about one-third has been published in collections.

2. Louis Kronenberger, *The Republic of Letters* (New York: Alfred A. Knopf, 1955), p. 249.

3. *A Writer's Diary*, ed. Leonard Woolf (New York: Harcourt Brace, 1953), p. 337.

4. "The Leaning Tower," *The Moment and Other Essays*, ed. Leonard Woolf (1st ed., 1947), reprint (London: Hogarth Press, 1964), p. 125.

5. *A Writer's Diary*, p. 172.

6. Woolf knew that the way people read depends on the age they belong to, but she could evoke the spirit of each age so strongly as to make her readers peripatetic through time. See "The Countess of Pembroke's Arcadia" and "The 'Sentimental Journey' " on Sidney's *Arcadia* and Sterne's *Sentimental Journey* in *The Common Reader*, 2d ser. (London: Hogarth Press, 1932).

7. "The Common Reader," *The Common Reader*, 1st ser. (Harvest ed.; New York: Harcourt, Brace, 1956), p. 1.

8. "Robinson Crusoe," *Common Reader*, 2d ser., p. 53.

9. "Mr. Bennett and Mrs. Brown," *The Captain's Death Bed*, ed. Leonard Woolf (London: Hogarth Press, 1950), pp. 103-4.

10. In considering whether or not Woolf is successful at making us identify with "we," the common reader, one should constantly remember how cautious Woolf herself was about claiming success. To her, the common reader was always an experiment, never a foregone conclusion. In entries for 1929, 1930, 1931, 1933, 1937, 1940, her diary contains constant self-doubts as she challenges herself to do better. See *Writer's Diary*, pp. 140, 156, 172, 203-4, 275, 324.

11. The process by which Woolf shaped her essays around key images can be pieced together through a reading of her ms. drafts, many of which can be found in the Berg Collection of the New York Public Library. It is fascinating. She would start out with a subject, begin writing down information and thoughts on it more or less at random, trying several different ways into it. As she rambled along, invariably an image would turn up. When it did, and if it was a good one, she would seize on it. From that moment, she would know she had the key to the essay it seems, for the essay's final form would usually be determined by the image's being placed at its opening, climax, end, or any combination of those.

12. *Common Reader*, 1st ser., pp. 40-48.

13. *A Writer's Diary*, p. 272.

14. "Oliver Goldsmith," *Captain's Death Bed*, p. 12.

15. "Henley's Criticism," *Times Literary Supplement*, February 24, 1921, p. 123.

16. "Sterne," *Granite and Rainbow*, ed. Leonard Woolf (London: Hogarth Press, 1960), p. 167; "The New Biography," ibid., p. 153.

17. *The Moment and Other Essays*, p. 138.

18. In an article called "Towards a Feminist History," *Female Studies V: Proceedings of the Conference Women and Education: A Feminist Perspective*, ed. Rae Lee Siporin (Pittsburgh: KNOW, 1972), pp. 49-52, Linda Gordon describes a radical new perspective on history which she illustrates at one point by writing, "Imagine, if you can, the story of the court of Louis XIV as told by one of his scullery maids, based on kitchen rumors and occasional glimpses of the lower edges of the court hierarchy." Virginia Woolf fostered just this kind of radical perspective on literature by emphasizing the role of affect in writing. She operated on the assumption that literature is not just the "great works," but is anything people write to fulfill themselves, whatever that means, in whatever way.

19. *A Writer's Diary*, p. 59.

20. Woolf's private point of view is as carefully hidden in her criticism as it is in her novels. In that sense, her achievement in one form is much the same as that in the other.

21. Aileen Pippett, *The Moth and the Star* (Boston: Little, Brown, 1953), p. 188.

22. "Outlines (II: Dr. Bentley)," *Common Reader*, 1st ser., p. 195.

23. "The Pastons and Chaucer," *Common Reader*, 1st ser., p. 14.

24. *A Room of One's Own* (New York: Harcourt, Brace, 1929), pp. 71-72.

25. Ibid., p. 52.

THEORIES OF FEMINIST CRITICISM:
A DIALOGUE

Carolyn Heilbrun & Catharine Stimpson

In the dialogue that follows, Heilbrun and Stimpson have isolated the essential differences between two distinct approaches to the feminist critical process, and presented them in the form of a debate between two feminist critics, designated "X" and "Y". Obviously, a certain amount of abstraction was necessary to develop the two positions as a working dialogue, and the two theories in fact complement rather than conflict with one another. The authors intend it to represent the sort of dialogue going on not only *among* feminists but within the individual feminist critic herself.

X: We do not so much disagree, perhaps, about what the feminist critic does, as about when she does it. That is why I want to speak a bit more of the extent to which we have isolated an area of disagreement. Malcolm Cowley, in writing of the generation of Americans who were to be known as "lost," spoke of how young writers were tempted to regard their own experience as negligible. "A Jewish boy from Brooklyn," Cowley wrote, might have behind him "representatives of the oldest Western culture now surviving. Behind him, too, lay memories of . . . the struggle of his parents against poverty, . . . all the emotions, smells and noises of the ghetto." But if his talent had won him a scholarship to college, "he would write . . . Keatsian sonnets about English abbeys, which he had never seen, and nightingales he had never heard." Women now face, and have long faced, the same situation, and they must learn to call upon their own experience, and the experience of women before them; they must learn not to be content to read "Keatsian sonnets about English abbeys" in the accepted way. Yet for the purposes of this dialogue, I am going to put aside what I know of the politics of literature, and suggest the ways in which even the despised New Criticism can become feminist criticism, the ways in which, in the light of feminist sensibilities, the text itself can reveal new meanings about human possibilities.

Y: I suppose that I begin as a textual archaeologist. I try to strip away layers of embedded attitudes and to dig up fragments of attitudes about sexuality, sex roles, their genesis, and their justifying ideologies. Two patterns most interest me now. The first is the presence of absence— hollows, centers, caverns within the work—places where activity that one might expect is missing. Menstruation, childbirth, or women's rage, for example, are events that are frequently absent from, or deceptively coded in literature. The second pattern is the sexualizing of the principle of activity, both exterior and interior, physical and mental. Literature has tended to masculinize most activity, particularly worldly activity, even as it has recorded it. The women in literature who try to act, or to exercise will, are by the books' denouements either prisoners or paralytics, literally or psychically. What tends to be considered aggressive and egocentric in a woman might as easily be considered a quest for liberty and self in a man.

I believe that we can trace and codify such patterns. They run through the various kinds of narrative: the realistic or roughly mimetic, satire, fantasy, irony, myth, and so on. They run all through drama and poetry. They run through film. One must learn to pick the clever, intricate locks of language that secure the more subtle secrets of narrative. I am still unsure of the number and kinds of differences that may emerge in the work of heterosexual men and women, homosexual men and women, and anonymous bards. Among the virtues of such archaeology is its scope. Not only are nearly all texts and verbal traces subject to scrutiny, but so are nearly, if not all, the persons and activities they dramatize. What, for example, is the nexus between sex and economics really like? To what degree does the affluent woman share in the freedom that is a necessary condition as well as a possible effect of autonomous activity, both as a character and as a writer?

That archaeology is neither to be separated from nor to be confused with advocacy. The work—perhaps simply the act of undertaking the work—implies a radical critique of our legacy of sex roles. The force of my advocacy tends to depend upon my audience. The substance of the critique remains the same, but the rhetoric changes from audience to audience. For example, before certain audiences, certain arguments may simply be assumed as common understanding.

X: You look for the ways in which women have *not* been represented in literature; you look for the absences, the stereotypes, the whole unfairness. And granted, this must be looked for. But once it has been identified, once our antennae have become very sensitive to the signs of women's belittlement, I think we must begin to look for the imaginative world that often lies unseen, at least in much literature. There is a distinction between what writers imagine and what they reflect. I search for what they imagine. You mention that literature has tended to masculinize most activity; you point out that what might be considered aggressive and egocentric in a woman might as easily be construed as a quest for liberty and self in a man. But if literature has masculinized activity, the compulsion to activity has often destroyed men, and literature has seen this too. The quest for liberty and self in a man has often forced him into aggressive and egocentric acts that destroy his self and endanger his world. I am less interested, finally, in how life limited the possibilities of action for Dorothea Brooke than in how failure to perceive the importance of Dorothea's value limited life for Lydgate.

Y: I am afraid of misunderstanding you. Do you mean that the failure of society to permit women a certain freedom, a failure that Eliot describes and Dorothea embodies, is less crucial than the failure of Lydgate to perceive Dorothea imaginatively, a failure that Eliot also describes? If you do mean that, then are you saying that the limitations of political and social structures are less vital than limitations of the individual imagination?

X: Vital for whom, and where? Obviously, society's failure toward women is of prime importance for the women's movement; how could it not be? But, once our consciousness is raised, we must begin to see imaginative patterns, archetypal patterns if you will, that reveal wherein the growth of moral perception lies. Anger is where we begin, but after we have expressed our anger, and recognized it, and turned it away from ourselves, to what do we turn our attention beyond the amelioration of social inequities? Few readers of *Middlemarch* today will fail to see how grievously life has crippled Dorothea. But how many will see as readily that Dorothea represents for Lydgate the consciousness toward which humanity, ideally, must move? The failure of society toward Dorothea is not less crucial than the failure of Lydgate to perceive Dorothea imaginatively, but it is more easily corrected, because it can be politically corrected. It may take years for awareness of servitude to develop, more years of hard political action for opportunities to develop. But the ability to see the range of those opportunities is the most difficult task of all; it is a task which, ideally, literature can serve.

Y: Your search, then, is for a new consciousness within the text. That consciousness may be new only in the sense that we, as readers, are seeing it for the first time. It will give us a way of perceiving society and ourselves in a fresher, freer way, and then for acting in a fresher, freer way. You are right to imply that, at the moment, I spend the greater part of my energy unearthing the patterns of the past and immediate present that literature reveals to us, rather than projecting a psychological, political, and moral Utopia for the future. From time to time I worry that my mode of feminist criticism will leave me in a cul-de-sac—a righteous one perhaps, but a cul-de-sac nonetheless. Although I fail to share that fear of anger in itself that Woolf expresses in *A Room of One's Own*, I also worry about becoming mired in anger. My criticism easily becomes a jeremiad, so that I become, as it were, too Old Testament—looking for the sins and errors of the past—a far more admonitory voice than yours.

X: All right; then I am New Testament—at least the New Testament of the Gospels. But I decline to be called Utopian. There is something dreamy and never-never-land about Utopias that I emphatically repudiate. But I will be brave enough to say that if you are Jeremiah, I am looking for the grace of imagination. A fine phrase, and what do I mean by it? I mean the grace to see what, until this moment, the masculinization of society has prevented us from seeing. We have all, until recently, been reading literature as though we were locked into the conventional male consciousness, whether or not we were men. Allowed into the male club of literary criticism, we women read all works in the light of the conventions of the male critic, who, of course, found only those things that his stringent ideas of maleness had taught him to look for. Not only did we ignore the absences you mention, the cries of rage; not only did we defend the sacrifice of women as only natural, and any defeat of men as life-denying, against the order of nature, to the extent that "to emasculate" became a synonym for "to kill"; but we also assumed that any male writer must be writing from the Freudian convictions of the male critics and professors who taught us. What I want to suggest as the grace of imagination functions in two ways. First, it functions somehow between what the author actually experiences and writes down in her/his notebooks, and the work of art s/he achieves. Second, it functions between the achieved work, the piece of literature, and the readers we have learned to be. A male writer may have imagined more than we were able to see before today; and we may now be able to see his works in a more open and symbolic way than we have been accustomed to reading them. If I may drag you into the New Testament with me for a moment: you have driven the moneychangers from the temple, while I suggest that virtue may dwell in unseen places, that the laws we have been taught may give way now to a new dispensation. We may understand that when Ibsen, James, Chekhov, Lawrence, Shaw, and Forster use a woman as the central consciousness in their works, they are doing so out of deep human impulse that has less to do with social justice than with their ideas of human possibility. The woman as hero was born, not from feminism, but from the author's realization that women at that moment best symbolized the human condition.

Y: But you mystify the imagination. You romanticize—and I use the word deliberately, to show a tradition as well as a trait—one particular mental faculty among several. I also romanticize the imagination. That is, I believe that the imagination, as it creates other worlds, gives us the simple sense of the possibility of a world other than the one we may inhabit, often to our discomfort and distaste. Even if there are only a set number of literary structures with which a writer can play, there is always enough new material at hand to create the sense of a fresh world. One of the reasons that one may criticize Joan Didion is her apparent refusal to construe a vision of the world that admits of flexibility, despite her claims to special expertise in moral ambiguities. I have less faith in the efficacy of the imagination to improve our lot in an everyday way than you do. On the other hand, I have more faith in our ability to understand the material conditions that breed creativity in some and prevent us from seeing it in others. The feminist critic should study the lives of the poets—sung and unsung. If personal and social biography does reveal the conditions under which creativity is released and appreciated, they might be incorporated into our personal and social organizations.

I wonder, too, if you are not relocating the moral authority once located in the church, the family, and the state in the exemplary text. You may be a neo-Arnoldian. I like that quality, because it openly declares that a text is a force, not an artifact; that a text may help to invigorate us. But isn't it true, though, that you discount the literary accounts that exist apart from the obvious "great" texts? Do you not dismiss things like my grandmother's letters simply because my grandmother's letters are not obviously among the best things that have been thought and written in our time? I wonder if we also disagree on the utility of "disinterestedness." Remember what Arnold writes in "The Function of Criticism": "How is criticism to show disinterestedness? By keeping aloof from what is called 'the practical view of things'; by resolutely following the law of its own nature, which is to be a free play of the mind on all subjects which it touches."

X: When you mention Arnold you reveal the horns of the dilemma on which you have me so neatly impaled. I admire disinterestedness profoundly, and mourn its loss in our world, a loss made evident by the misuse of the word *dis*interested to mean *un*interested. I think that the best approach to literature, finally, *is* aloof from the practical view of things, is, as Joyce said, static rather than kinetic. Yet who can be unaware how long the supposed virtue of disinterestedness has been imposed on women readers of literature, how long it has prevented women from seeing how imprisoned they have been. There are virtues that come only with strength and power, and disinterestedness is such a virtue. If we study literature in the light of history, then we must of course read your grandmother's letters. But when we study literature nonhistorically, we can afford to be less practical. Once we have seen all the practical views of women's disability, and the narrow imagination of many writers, then, *then*, we must look, disinterestedly, for the miracles imagination has wrought; miracles, because they can be neither explained nor anticipated. We must then, I believe, stop teaching people, as you advocate, and begin teaching *literature*, as I advocate. Whereas you see Oedipus's tragedy as the tragedy of will, as a male tragedy, I see it as embodying a quintessential human movement, from purpose to perception, a movement available to all humanity, undergone alike by Oedipus *and* Mrs. Alving. When I look at *Tom Jones*, however, I have no trouble seeing the women as stereotyped, as commodities, and, having learned from you to see these things, move on to *Clarissa* where, it seems to me, a more broadly human tragic pattern unfolds.

Y: The metaphor of horns tends to stagger me. It implies a binary, either/or view of the world and of modes of behavior. The feminist critic is capable of simultaneous actions, disinterestedness *and* advocacy. That simultaneity is also capable of being misunderstood. I do distinguish between the feminist critic and the critic who does feminist criticism from time to time. Very soon now, the various techniques of feminist criticism will be charted. Like French or Esperanto, they will comprise a language that a person may practice and learn, learn and practice, without having it affect his or her actions outside of the study or classroom. Consider this hypothetical possibility: a person gives a perceptive paper about *Middlemarch*. S/he shows the complex ironies of the final passage, in which Dorothea, a model for the growth of consciousness, becomes a model of the sacrificial dissipation of energies, of energies used to fertilize the soil in which others flourish. Then my hypothetical person tapdances into a departmental meeting and votes against a qualified woman simply because she is a woman. That would be a case of a critic simply practicing feminist criticism. An authentic feminist critic, on the other hand, would also act to end the deplorable patterns s/he had graphed. As I say these things, I feel as if I were a mouthpiece for truisms.

Your comment about tragedy also interests me. I *am* convinced that our theories of tragedy have been largely masculinized. Tragedy (despite extraordinary exceptions, like *Hamlet*) rises like smoke out of that destructive gap between action and consciousness, between will and a deep understanding of the consciousness of will, between inadvertently killing one's father and knowing who one's father is. The tragic pattern for women, too often unrecognized, is the reverse. Tragedy, for many women characters, springs from the fact that consciousness must outpace the possibilities of action, that perception must pace within an iron cage. Women writers, like Charlotte Brontë, have been very quick to see the limits of action open to, as well as permissible for, women. To oversimplify, the tragic man acts before he thinks; the tragic woman thinks and knows she cannot act. Look at Lily Bart in *The House of Mirth*. She sees her life more and more clearly. Ironically, the more clearly she sees, the more deeply she knows that her life cannot change for the better. To be fair, *The House of Mirth* may be a bad example. Wharton's world is apparently too deterministic to allow anyone, male or female, the opportunity for personal transfiguration.

X: I want to go back and pick up some points. We both become mouthpieces for truisms, because when it comes to advocacy, we agree. Our argument lies after advocacy. One *can* take a binary view of feminist criticism, I think, if only to the extent that—I cannot seem to keep away from the Bible, and will now join you in the Old Testament—after your feminist critic has led us to the promised land, my feminist critic must enter it and see it as the promised land for humanity, the Egypt of female servitude having been left behind. Your point about someone practising my sort of feminist criticism and following it by a vote against a woman because she is a woman seems to me unfair. Hypocrisy is never admirable, nor the inability to translate one's perceptions into actions. But I do not believe that a critic trained to see that Henry Wilcox in *Howards End* is not "gelded," as we have been taught, but undergoes a rebirth no less vital because we are unused to seeing men undergo such rebirths—no critic trained to see this will vote against a woman on grounds of her sex alone unless he is a hypocrite, in which case, why are we discussing him?

Y: Because he/she exists, because he/she will continue to exist, and because he/she must be dealt with. You underestimate the persistence of the breed.

X: They will be no easier to deal with, now or in the future, if we refrain from my feminist criticism. We must always cope with bigots, in Egypt, in the desert, and in the promised land. But their strength and power is altered, and weakened, by us both.

One other point you made, a long way back, was the importance of studying what you call the lives of the poets. I want to say that here too, we must make a distinction between the content of "women's courses" and the work of the literary critic. Courses in biography should certainly spend more time on the letters and diaries of women, rather than on the lives of so-called men of action. But if we look at literature as a text of human possibility, we may begin to see something new.

Here I return for a moment to Dorothea, whom you describe as "a model for the sacrificial dissipation of energies, energies used to fertilize the soil in which others grow." I dislike that word "dissipation," with its implication of waste. Many use their energies, and choose to use them, "to fertilize the soil in which others grow." Such a destiny should not be scorned. Its only shame lies in its being seen as a destiny possible only to women and slaves. If Lydgate represents those persons who doom themselves to a dreadful situation because they discover, too late, the evil in stereotyping, so Dorothea represents those who, choosing to serve, are granted no decent sphere in which to do so. But once we have learned the feminist advocacy point—that women ought not to have such confined destinies—we go on to the literary point, which says that full humanity is lost to both sexes where value cannot be openly perceived.

As to tragedy, it seems to me here that the sex of the tragic hero is, beyond advocacy, a matter of some indifference. Is it not the human pattern to conceive the illusion that we can control destiny, suffer for it until the will is lost, and so become aware? Like Oedipus, heroes become redeemers when the will is burned out, when the Tiresean vision replaces the vision of arrogant sightedness. You see will and action as masculinized, but will and action are human, and, since all humans act necessarily from partial knowledge, there is a degree to which all persons must perceive will and action to have been mistaken. This seems to me to be where feminist criticism, beyond advocacy, can lead us. Lily Bart, deprived of the possibility of action, is not a tragic hero: she is a societal fact.

Y: I need some clarification of terms here. I find it hard to accept your description of Lily Bart as a societal fact, as if she were simply an unfortunate statistic.

X: The tragic hero is distinguished from the societal fact in that his/her passion is undergone not because of a social evil that can be remedied, but because of the limitations inherent in being human. If Lily Bart is a societal fact, the same might be said of Mailer's machismo types. Both Lily Bart and the Mailer hero are entrapped in a prison of gender, and neither speaks for humanity, except to reveal its societal mistakes. The tragic pattern, on the other hand, is available to all, whether perceived through Mrs. Alving or Oedipus. The realization that "perception has outpaced the possibility of action" is not a tragedy peculiar to women, but the tragedy of anyone, man or woman, who sees too late that perception must precede action. Circumstance can render action impossible for any of us, or at least can place an extraordinary price upon it. I would challenge you by suggesting that your ideal is male action made available to women, while for me the ideal is awareness, and the knowledge of the human price of action, however necessary it may be. You want a female Faust, and I want a male Antigone.

Y: If we are to construe *Antigone* as a conflict between the authority of the state and the authority of conscience, we have had male Antigones, and we have celebrated them. Look, for example, at the figure of Orestes in *The Flies*. And if we are to construe a female Faust as a smart and bold figure, then I suppose I do want one. However, if we are to construe Faust as a paradigm of overarching ambition, I would not particularly celebrate a female version. (Needless to say, I hardly celebrate the Eternal Feminine.) I admire the poetry of Plath, but the *persona* the poetry creates often troubles me. She is, in many ways, a female Faust. The no-holds wrestling with death is a Faustian risk.

In general, I am charier and warier than you about the promised land. I have not yet constructed its geography to my satisfaction except as a negation of much of the geography of the present and as a place in which a few, time-worn axioms—e.g., we must love one another or die; adult sex must be a matter of private choice between consenting adults—are acted out. What should the new criteria for human success be? Perhaps my timidity in constructing a promised land is little more than fear of error.

X: There is no such thing as a feminine Faust, so we need do nothing with Plath in this connection. The wrestle with death is not Faustian; Faust is beyond death and trades his soul for knowledge, a masculine myth of the Western world. Faust is what happens when man, males, have too much power, find life too easy, use women too lightly, and seek for extra sensation. Faust tells of a world of distortion. Plath wrestled with death as Jacob wrestled with the angel, as every woman wrestles with the terrible seduction of non-being in the face of have-to-be. Between Faust and Plath lie centuries of sexualized human experience.

Y: Think of the poetry of Plath in another way. Think of that lightning, nervy voice crying out for non-being simply as a transition to a greater being.

X: The way of non-being is never chosen by Faust.

Y: Perhaps non-being is a misleading phrase. Plath sometimes describes death as oblivion, but she also describes it in terms of sensation. The point I am trying to make about her dramas is their quality of risk. I also want to go back to amplify some earlier points. One reason that I praise letters, diaries, and other homely genres is that they may offer, in their realistic notation of what a life was like as it was lived, the same sense of possibility that you find in great, imaginative texts. Women who coped with actual demands, pressures, and events were often tough and resilient. As they carried on, they created, without much literary self-consciousness, a mode of action that was at once ingenious and humane. I believe we see such modes in what black women have said about themselves, when they use language as a medium of self-description, not as the medium for a text of another world.

My attitude towards Mailer, as one example of a virility freak, is simple. Writers who expand consciousness are good. Their texts perform the function of a safety valve. As I read them, I have a sense of an event without having to endure it. Reading Mailer gives me a vicarious experience of violence. It reinforces my hatred of violence without having to become its bruised and battered victim. Mailer also has verbal and psychic energy. He teaches us about the joy and value of releasing energy. Finally, though he can be dogmatic and authoritarian himself, he is skeptical of much received authority. Skepticism of authority is like a contagious disease. Since most structures of authority are masculine, to question them *per se* may lead us to question masculine authority *per se*. In *Bleak House*, when Dickens dissects the murky labyrinths of the court, he effectively dissects the men who both run them—and run within them.

X: I like your explanations of Mailer's uses. Born when I was, I never felt I needed an example of virility consciousness in literature, life having provided plenty; that you do may be the most hopeful thing said here yet. What we need now is to give *men* the vicarious experience of renunciation and awareness; this has never been attempted because men will not pay attention to many so-called women's novels. I am thus less interested, from a literary point of view, in women's personal letters than I am in involving men in what is defined as the female experience of perception, as opposed to aggression and violence. I am ready to use the literature of the world to train men to read themselves, rather than only to train women to notice how unheard or exploited they have been. The masculine avoidance of what we have come to call the feminine experience seems to me far more destructive to our world today that the feminine avoidance of what we have come to call the masculine experience, because violence and the love of action is learned more easily than either awareness or love. Let us say that you, with your advocacy, will teach women the joys of action and I, with my disinterestedness, will teach men the joys of awareness. For a degree of passivity is not in itself evil; it is evil only when it is demanded from half of humanity. We must be free to range ourselves on the spectrum of human action for reasons other than that of gender. The features of the promised land are no clearer to me than they are to you; but it will be a place where literary perceptions will avail past the necessity of social action.

Y: Whenever I talk about feminist criticism, I am amazed at how high a moral tone I take.

X: If your tone is high, mine is lost somewhere in the stratosphere. I want to seize the last word to say how aware I am that I have built my ideal feminist criticism, as men have been wont to do, on the hard work of women. But unlike men, I acknowledge the debt and know that without your feminist criticism, there would be no foundation for mine.

AFTERWORD: CRITICAL RE-VISION

Josephine Donovan

> Re-vision—the act of looking back,
> of seeing with fresh eyes, of entering
> an old text from a new critical direction—
> is for us more than a chapter in cultural
> history: it is an act of survival.[1]

While in practice feminist critics continue to use a variety of methodological approaches to literature, there are common assumptions that
underlie a feminist approach to anything. It is upon this commonality
that I wish to dwell, so as to place feminist literary criticism within the
context of a more general critical theory.

Feminists believe that women have been locked off in a condition of
lesser reality by the dominant patriarchal attitudes and customs of our
culture. We find these attitudes and customs reified in the institutions
of literature and literary criticism. Feminist critics—like feminists in
every area—are engaged in negating these reifications.

Thus, I believe that we may describe feminist criticism as a mode of
negation seen within a fundamental dialectic. For there is a fundamental transformation of consciousness taking place at this time in
history, and the women's movement is a, if not *the*, critical part of this
change.

The contributors to this collection implicitly intend this dialectic in
their theories. Register, for example, uses the term "prescriptive criticism" to describe what she believes may become the defining attribute
of feminist criticism in the future, that is, "criticism [which] attempts
to set standards for literature . . . from a feminist viewpoint. It is
prescriptive in that it implies a need for new literature that meets its
standards" (see p. 2 above).

If I may expand slightly on this definition to clarify my own thesis, criticism is here viewed as a vehicle through which literature is prescriptively related to its social, cultural, and moral environment. The prescriptive critic relates literature to changes that are occurring in the structure of human consciousness, in the patterns of identification by which we organize our social, cultural, and moral reality. This kind of criticism requires that the critic be sensitive to the formation of new patterns, as the process is occurring. It proposes, at the same time, a critic who is not indifferent to the changes that are taking place. Indeed, the "prescriptive" critic is actively engaged in encouraging the social and cultural realization of those structural changes that promote human liberation. Prescriptive criticism exists in what sociologists call the "prophetic" mode.[2]

Herbert Marcuse articulates a demand for the kind of critical awareness prescriptive criticism entails in several of his works, notably *One Dimensional Man* and *Eros and Civilization*. He calls it the "power of negative thinking."[3] Like most male theorists Marcuse has until quite recently failed to take the women's movement seriously. Nevertheless, his perceptions on the dialectics of liberation are relevant to our struggle.

Marcuse is saying, in Hegelian tradition, that the human consciousness has the power to say no to the status quo in the name of values that are not realized in the conditions of existing society. Following Heidegger, he argues that today's existing reality is one of lesser ontological status, one of lesser being. Yet, through the modes of Logos and Eros, "two modes of negation," the human consciousness can "break the hold of the established, contingent reality and strive for a truth incompatible with it."[4] Out of this critical dialectic will emerge a transcending synthesis.

I believe that feminist criticism may be seen as a mode of "negative thinking" in Marcuse's sense of the term. Unlike an Hegelian, however, I am unclear whether our negations will lead to the promised synthetic end. (Nor am I sure that we would want them to.) I doubt that we will ever see the convergence so dreamed of in the contemporary philosophical imagination.[5]

Nonetheless, I feel that our negations will at least make way for the workings of what one might call imaginative "grace," so named by another contributor to this collection; that is, "the grace to see what, until this moment, the masculinization of society has prevented us from seeing" (see Heilbrun and Stimpson, p. 64 above). This itself may yield transcending visions.

Thus, as feminist critics, our sensitivities must be negative in that we are saying no to a whole series of oppressive ways, images, and false-hoods that have been perpetrated against women both in literature and in literary criticism. But, on the other hand, we must be sensitive, too, to the new imaginative perceptions, to the new shapes that are begin-ning to take form—partly as a result of our negations.

We must be sensitive to new orders of facts and realities, new consciousness forms.[6] And, as we become aware of these new shapes, however "touch'd but faintly" they may be, we ourselves have new models through which to see literary texts. Aspects of literature that we have never seen before light up as we approach through the focals of our new perspective models.[7]

Not only, however, are we involved in the recognition of new "paradigms" (following Thomas Kuhn's terminology[8]); we are, as femi-nist critics, involved in their creation. The new feminist critic is not "disinterestedly" describing cultural phenomena in the tradition of academic liberalism. She is (and knows herself to be) politically moti-vated by a concern to redeem women from the sloughbin of nonentity in which they have languished for centuries. Her procedure, then, is to propose a critique of the literary and critical structures that have held women in a condition of lesser reality in both the past and the present. The determination of what those structures are derives more perhaps from feminism as a political theory than it does from theories of literary criticism.

The feminist critic is saying, moreover, that each person "sees" phenomena through a filter of concerns and awarenesses; we feminist critics recognize these in ourselves and so at least come to the critical dialogue in relative good faith. For this reason we pose a challenge to the assumption that any scholar is free from ideological bias or value preference.

Many of the contributors to this volume see the concept of androgyny as an important paradigm that feminist and humanist critics will be assuming in future work. Another series of concepts likely to be developed in the next several years revolves around the concept of a female culture. Radical feminists and lesbians have been in the fore-front of the women's movement in seeking the patterns that identify women as a separate cultural group. Out of these as yet embryonic tendencies may emerge a feminist, or feminine, aesthetic.[9] As of now it is premature to say what such an aesthetic may entail.

Nonetheless, it is already clear that one of the primary criteria by which feminist critics are judging works of literature is by what one might call the "truth criterion" (see Holly's essay, pp. 38-47 above). That is, we are making judgments based on an assessment of the authenticity of women characters, women's situations, and the authors' perspective on them. Such judgments may be based in large part on the critic's own experience as a woman, but also upon the new awarenesses of the female experience that have come and are still coming to light through the women's movement.

The feminist critic maintains, in short, that there are truths and probabilities about the female experience that form a criterion against which to judge the authenticity of a literary statement about women. Beyond this, critics are also judging what one might call the perspective of a writer according to similar sex-based criteria—that is, characterizing a writer's perspective or vision as being excessively masculine, or as serving a male supremacist ideology (as Kate Millett characterized Mailer, Miller, and Lawrence in *Sexual Politics*).

This latter direction implies an awareness of what a feminine per-spective entails, or what a whole, androgynous vision might entail. My own feeling is that the immediate work in feminist criticism must be to develop more fully our understanding of what a female perspective or vision includes. Through information gleaned from research in women's studies, I see a gradual falling together of truths and probabilities about women—their experience, their history, their wisdom, their culture—and this constellation will provide the basis for a feminine aesthetic. As our concept of what constitutes the female identity, and female society and culture, becomes clearer, we will be better able to appreciate works of art and literature in terms of its configurations. In other words, I believe that there is a female culture which we must retrieve, and we must begin to articulate criteria of judgment that are consonant with the wisdom and experience of womankind, as developed and transmitted through the ages.

As an example, consider the fact that male critics have often dismissed women writers and their subjects as trivial or minor. This is because male critics have not been sensitive to certain realities and perceptions that are common to women. But in order to counter the male charges, we have to refine and substantiate our sense of what we mean by "women's reality" or "women's perspectives."

One writer who has continually explored this female dimension is Anaïs Nin. In her writing she takes for granted certain assumptions about female sensitivity. One may agree or disagree with those assumptions (I for the most part agree); but if a feminine aesthetic is to be established, a consensus of what these assumptions are has to take shape.

The following passage from Nin's *The Future of the Novel* is a good example of a female critic defending a woman writer (Djuna Barnes) against a male critic's derogations by asserting the validity of the feminine vision.

> [There] is nothing effete about *Nightwood* unless Mr. Guérard so defines feminine writing. Djuna Barnes dealt with the anguish of love instead of the horrors of destruction and sadism. Possibly because I also dealt with love and not with cruelty, I was labeled effete, precious, esoteric, and strange. And so what William Goyen wittily called "the motorcycle-leather pseudomasculinity" is carefully nurtured by certain male critics, and the perversions of sadism in John Hawkes' work are admired while the studies of love and its erratic course as in *Nightwood* and *Miss MacIntosh, My Darling* are still not fully and justly evaluated. . . . [A] false masculinity has made critics unaware of feminine writers. There are many states and sensations which defy barracks language and which are done masterfully by women writers.[10]

Until we have had a chance to study women's art, history, and culture more extensively, so as to begin to codify the patterns of consciousness delineated therein, I believe we will be unable to develop a more substantial feminine aesthetic. For aesthetic judgments are rooted in epistemology: one cannot understand why someone thinks something is beautiful or significant until one understands the way s/he *sees,* knows the world.

In his essay on "African-Negro Aesthetics" Leopold Senghor devotes considerable attention to the question of how the black person sees, knows and relates to the world:

[The] Negro is [not] . . . devoid of reason. . . . But his reason is not discursive; it is synthetic. It is not antagonistic, but sympathetic. This is another path to knowledge. Negro reason does not impoverish things. It does not mold them into rigid categories, eliminating the juices and the sap; it flows into the arteries of things. . . . White reason is analytical through use. Negro reason is intuitive through participation.[11]

By establishing black epistemology Senghor lays a foundation for an understanding of black aesthetics. We must establish more substantially what women's knowledge is, if we are to establish a female aesthetic.

Beyond a critique of content, however, there are methodological changes which we might expect in the wake of the development of a feminine aesthetic. I suspect, for example, following Virginia Woolf, that a feminine aesthetic will call for "less. . . 'system' and more sympathy" (see Bell and Ohmann, p. 50 above). That is to say, a feminine aesthetic will provide for the integration into the critical process of the experiences denoted as "feminine" in our culture.

It may, in fact, be less "criticism" and more "appreciation." No longer will our literature be mediated by the hollow men Virginia Woolf describes as stabbing at literary texts as if at "noxious insects" (p. 59 above). Instead, we critics will, as teachers, embrace the reader on common ground and approach the work together. No longer will we accept the totalitarian dogma of the formalists that there is but one way to read a text,[12] that criticism must be concerned with filtering out "irrelevant" responses, as I. A. Richards proposed. Instead, we will recognize that critics and readers are whole persons who come to literature with tunnels of experience through which they view the happenings of the text. We will recognize that much of literary appreciation is a personal subjective experience, and that to brush off such responses as irrelevant is only to perpetuate the destructive antinomies drawn in the Western cultural identity: between personal and public, emotional and intellectual, subjective and objective.

Perhaps criticism will become collective: perhaps we will share our perceptions and responses in group situations, not worrying to sort them out into linear logic for one-dimensional consumption through our professional journals, but rather coming forth with multi-strata readings that tell us as much about one another as they do about the text. (I believe it significant that two of the pieces in this collection are collaborative efforts.) Or, perhaps criticism will become more subjective, personal, or impressionistic—that is, critics will share personal perceptions and insights; the best critics will be those whose reading is the most extensive and whose range and depth of understanding is the most distinctive. Perhaps we will find that personal ˄ssays, such as those by Virginia Woolf herself, are more congenial to the female sensibility.

There are, of course, many problems to be worked out. But, in the end our vision is integral. We do not believe that one can separate literature from life any more than we believe that a critic can separate her/himself from her/his social, cultural and personal identity.

For this reason much of the theorizing about feminist criticism has involved thinking about pedagogy and about the nature of higher education today. We know, as Fraya Katz-Stoker has pointed out, that "literature is a major component of the educational process, and that process, not biological determinism, shapes our destiny."[13]

Katz-Stoker argues that criticism is finally the teaching of literature. Feminist criticism is finally the teaching of literature to persons with certain ends in view. We have seen that those ends involve the negation of certain reified falsehoods about women and the establishment of new consciousness forms and new social and cultural orders that will allow women, indeed all humans, to grow to their fullest potential.

The feminist critic is thus on the cutting edge of the dialectic. She must, in a sense be Janus-headed: engaged in negations that yield transcendences. The requisite negative attitude is the one that Mary Daly demanded of all feminists: "What is required of women at this point in history is a firm and deep refusal to limit our perspectives, questioning, and creativity to any of the preconceived patterns of male-dominated culture."[14]

Beyond negations we must move toward and into transcending consciousness. The dynamic of the women's movement—like all historical transformations of consciousness—is dialectical. As feminist critics we must be faithful to this dynamic and engaged in its process.

NOTES

1. Adrienne Rich, "When We Dead Awaken: Writing as Re-Vision," *College English* 34 (October 1972):18.

2. So labeled by Robert Friedrichs in *A Sociology of Sociology* (Free Press, 1970): "This tradition ... defines the sociologist as a critic of society, an engaged, committed scholar who seeks to influence the future through his analysis of the present." See *Humanistic Sociology*, ed. John F. Glass and John R. Staude (Pacific Palisades, California: Goodyear, 1972), p. xii.

3. Herbert Marcuse, *One Dimensional Man* (Boston: Beacon, 1964), p. 11.

4. Ibid., p. 127.

5. See William I. Thompson, "The Individual As Institution," *Harper's Magazine*, September 1972, pp. 48-62, for a discussion of current theories of convergence–those of Paolo Soleri, Teilhard de Chardin, Marshall McLuhan, and others. I think that the theory of androgyny may be considered a theory of convergence.

6. For further discussion of this point see Ginny Foster, "Women as Liberators," *Female Studies VI: Closer to the Ground*, ed. Nancy Hoffman, Cynthia Secor, and Adrian Tinsley (Old Westbury, New York: The Feminist Press, 1972).

7. A good example of this kind of criticism is Carolyn Heilbrun's *Toward a Recognition of Androgyny* (New York: Alfred A. Knopf, 1973) in which the critic looks through the model "androgyny" and in a whole series of past works sees patterns that simply had not been seen or understood before. See also Annis Pratt's reinterpretation to *To the Lighthouse* in terms of the androgyny concept in "Sexual Imagery in *To the Lighthouse:* A New Feminist Approach," *Modern Fiction Studies* 18(Autumn 1972):417-31.

8. See Thomas Kuhn, *The Structure of Scientific Revolutions* (Chicago: University of Chicago Press, 1970).

9. I think one may distinguish between a *feminist* aesthetic and a *feminine* one. The former derives judgments from ideological assumptions; the latter would derive from a sense of female epistemology as rooted in authentic female culture.

10. Anaïs Nin, *The Future of the Novel* (New York: Collier, 1968), pp. 178-79.

11. *The Ideology of Blackness*, ed. Raymond F. Betts (Lexington, Mass.: D. C. Heath, 1971), p. 111. There are interesting similarities between Senghor's characterization of black knowledge and Robert Jay Lifton's perceptions of women's knowledge. See Robert Jay Lifton, "Woman As Knower," *The Woman in America*, ed. Lifton (Boston: Beacon, 1967), pp. 27-51. See also Nin, *The Future of the Novel*, p. 75.

12. The ideological bias of most practicing critics has been identified by Frederick Crews in "Do Literary Studies Have An Ideology?" *PMLA* 85, no. 3 (May 1970):427-28: "The critic's relation to his text is manipulative rather than involved. Instead of accepting and examining the temperamental affinity that led him to treat a certain author, he displays his capacity to perform correct and efficient operations that will give him total possession of the work. . . . It is like the computerized pacification of a province." While Crews sees this mentality as being imperialistic, coming out of the final phases of monopolistic capitalism, he fails to note the male psychology involved in the idea of totally subduing a work to one's own critical categories.

13. Fraya Katz-Stoker, "The Other Criticism: Feminism vs. Formalism," *Images of Women in Fiction, Feminist Perspectives*, ed. Susan Koppelman Cornillon (Bowling Green, Ohio: Bowling Green University Popular Press, 1972), p. 324.

14. Mary Daly, *Beyond God The Father, Toward a Philosophy of Women's Liberation* (Boston: Beacon, 1973), p. 7.

CONTRIBUTORS

Barbara Currier Bell is assistant professor of English at Wesleyan University. She holds a Ph.D. from Columbia University.

Josephine Donovan teaches in the Honors Program at the University of Kentucky. She received her doctorate in comparative literature from the University of Wisconsin.

Carolyn Heilbrun is professor of English at Columbia University, and the author of *Toward a Recognition of Androgyny, Christopher Isherwood, The Garnett Family,* and numerous reviews and articles.

Marcia Holly is the editor of the forthcoming collection of essays on women and literature, *Patterns of Strength.*

Carol Ohmann is associate professor and chairperson of the department of English at Wesleyan University. She is the author of *Ford Madox Ford: From Apprentice to Craftsman*, as well as articles on English and American fiction.

Cheri Register is assistant professor at the University of Minnesota. She received her doctorate from the University of Chicago where she did her thesis on feminist literary criticism.

Dorin Schumacher is a member of the faculty at the University of Maine at Orono, and holds a Ph.D. from the University of Pittsburgh.

Catharine Stimpson is associate professor of English at Barnard College, and the author of *J. R. R. Tolkien* and essays on modern and postmodern literature.